The Beer's Folded and the Laundry's Cold:

Mostly-True Adventures in Housewifery

Paige Kellerman

Cover Design by Scott Brooks
Edited by Brenda Errichiello
Formatted by Polgarus Studio

For My Children.

You changed everything, and I like that.

Contents

Introduction 1

Chapter 1 I Will Never Get Married 3

Chapter 2 Tightening the Old Belt 15

Chapter 3 To Get Dressed or Not to Get Dressed 27

Chapter 4 I'm Just a Girl, Standing in Front of a Mixer, Asking It to be a Paperweight 37

Chapter 5 Breaking News: Pinterest Threatens to Make Drinkers (or worse drinkers) of Homemakers Everywhere. 53

Chapter 6 The New Ikea Catalog Says Placing the Kitchen Sink By a Window Makes Doing Dishes More Fun. It's Also a Good Reminder of the Futility of Escape. 65

Chapter 7 Bills, Bills, Bills 77

Chapter 8 Everyone Can Just Go Naked 89

Chapter 9 I'd Like to See Someone In HR About the Benefits Package 99

Chapter 10 Cleanliness is Next To Insanity 111

Chapter 11 A Day of the Week, By Any Other Name, Is Still a Monday 125

Chapter 12 And Then We Just Stared At Each Other. 137

Chapter 13 Yours, Mine, Our Money.......................... 149

Chapter 14 The Time I Tried to Take A Sick Day 161

Chapter 15 A Quick Dinner.. 173

Chapter 16 A Letter To Store Owners, From A Vampire.. 177

Chapter 17 All My Friends Live In the Computer 183

Chapter 18 If It Breaks, I Buy It................................. 193

Chapter 19 What Do You Do All Day? 209

Acknowledgments..217

Housewife:

Someone who cooks delicious meals, does laundry with a smile, and wears high heels while she vacuums.

Housewifery: When Paige Kellerman attempts to do any of the above.

Introduction

I know what you're thinking. "An introduction? Only people completely full of themselves put introductions in books. If she thinks she's that fancy, maybe I should return this book and get my money back. In fact, I could've bought a pretty nice sized burrito bowl at Chipotle with that money instead. Yeah, that's what I'll do. I'll buy a burrito bowl."

I'll be honest with you: procuring reasonably priced chicken, beans and optional guacamole is actually a great plan, but I hope you'll decide to stick around. (Or, if you do go, bring me back a Corona with lime.) You and me, we're about to go on a journey full of wonderful things, like burning dinner and trying not to overdraft the checking account. This isn't a rant about needing to be barefoot and pregnant in the kitchen, although I've been barefoot and pregnant in the kitchen a few times because I hate shoes, get pregnant by *looking* at my husband, and because that's where we keep the cookies. Actually, I'm also barefoot in the dining room, holding a toddler who's yelling, "It's me again!", while I type, so…technicalities. This is the story of a girl who worked in an office and then didn't work in an office. A girl who thought no effort at all went into rearing children or running a house. A girl who thought wearing sweatpants with clever sayings printed on the butt was the height of fashion, but changed her ways before it was too late and Yves St Lauren found and hit her with a tractor.

Neither a manifesto nor a "how-to," this book is simply the tale of how a hidden set of circumstances I didn't know existed unfolded before me—and how I flicked cigarette butts at those circumstances until I could formulate a proper, adult response. I've never enjoyed the term "season of life," mostly because I live in Kansas, and the seasons here are a never-ending winter. However, "season" is probably the best way to explain this stage of my life, the season of comforting children who fall on their face for no reason and the season of trying to make money stretch like a two-dollar pair of pantyhose. The future may very well find me back in the office, and that's ok, but until then, I'll be trying to remember to cook with more than one ingredient, to only drink after bedtime, and to keep the floors clean enough to safely set a chair on, without it sticking to the laminate. So thank you again for picking up this book. Grab a drink (the following pages pair well with anything containing an alcohol volume over five percent), and let's get to it.

Sincerely,
Paige

Chapter 1

I Will Never Get Married

The year was 2006 and things were good. My abs were flat, my hair was being trimmed regularly, and *The Lake House* was out in theatres. The thing I was most sure of—second to the fact that Sandra Bullock and Keanu Reeves had intentionally created one of the most confusing movies ever—was the fact I'd never get married.

One evening, while sitting on top of my parents' dining room table, I held up my spoon and made a solemn declaration. "I'm never getting married."

My mom stopped wiping the table around me. "Why's that?"

Pushing the Rocky Road around in my bowl, I thought for a second before I answered. "It's too much trouble." Setting down my spoon, I ticked the reasons off on my fingers. "Finding the right person. Getting to know the right person. Convincing them to stay with you for life despite the fact you smoke a pack a day, watch *Bridget Jones's Diary* on a regular basis, and pick the remote control up off the floor with your feet? Impossible."

She nodded knowingly. "I see. Well, don't be surprised

if you end up finding someone you get along with. You've always struck me as the marrying type, and I'm sure there are tons of guys out there who'd love to get to know you." She was quiet for minute. "Do you really smoke a pack a day? You're only twenty-two."

I shrugged. "Is that even a type? Listen, I'm happy working in insurance. I'll work my way up, move somewhere exotic that has a thriving insurance need, and live happily by myself. I'm not trying to dash your hopes of grandchildren, but most of the guys I've met up to this point have the personality of a ham sandwich."

"So, you're not getting married?"

Assessing the melting ice cream situation in the bottom of my bowl, I poked a marshmallow island and sighed. "I will never get married." And that was that. I drank the rest of my chocolate, dropped my bowl in the sink, and went home to watch *Bridget Jones's Diary.*

Two years later, I looked at the boy with shaggy brown hair who was asking me if I would marry him, and I said, "Yes." And, "Also, are you going to eat the rest of those mashed potatoes?" (I know, I know. Lifelong commitment had previously been off the table, but when someone takes the time to buy you the entire *Time-Life Collection Ten Disk Set: Sounds of the Seventies* for Christmas, you don't think about it. You marry them.)

He smiled and nudged the ring box closer to my plate so I wouldn't forget to take it with me. "Yes, I am."

Excitedly, I brandished my fork. "Hmm, that's too bad because sharing everything starts with this side dish. What about your steak?"

Ten months, three kegs, and only one noise complaint to the police about the reception later, we were hitched and headed for a honeymoon in Florida. After that, there was only one un-enthused dolphin sighting, two months, and five minutes to figure out where to store the new gin glasses, and then we were expecting twins. Again, I perched on my parents' kitchen table, raised my spoon, and made profound declarations.

"I'll never stay home."

My mother continued sorting and paying various bills we'd racked up for her over the years. "And why's that?"

"It's just not for me. That and I really don't think we have the money to do anything of the kind. Not to mention the fact I have a thriving career in insurance."

She nudged a water bill aside. "I thought you hated your job."

"Hate is such a strong word. I prefer 'like a little more than I love camping.'"

"But you hate camping."

"Exactly. But insurance pays the bills, and who doesn't love having their head anchored to their desk by a stylish-yet-practical headset?"

The fact was I wasn't crazy about my job, but the money was good, and with two babies on the way, money was a must. Rumor had it call centers had a certain charm, but I'd yet to find it while logging numerous conversations about why I could or could not help other people with their requests for insurance or whether failing to stop at a stoplight should be considered a moving violation in states that had "Live Free and Die Young" as their motto.

"But the light was really more of a rose color than an actual red."

"Did it have any shades of green to it?" I'd ask.

"No."

"You're sure? Not even the slightest hint of chartreuse?"

"Nope."

"Well then, auto insurance may be problem for you. But we'll be happy to send you a free color wheel with your rejection letter."

Growing up, I'd pictured my adult life as a mix of circus performer, magician, and florist. Unfortunately, dreams such as these tend to fizzle out once one realizes sawing oneself in half takes a body double and mirrors that exceed the everyday budget. Also that crafting a wedding bouquet only when inspiration strikes might not pay the rent. I needed something lucrative. Being the realist I was, I'd recognized this early and decided I'd pick a more reliable dream, go get my degree in English, and become a writer instead.

My mother's excitement had been palpable. "Umm, that's really great. In the meantime, what were you planning on doing for money?"

I waved off her skepticism with what I perceived to be a vast amount of natural talent. "Why, write the next great American novel, woman. What else?"

"Will you be eating this great American novel?"

"Of course not. It's impossible to eat something encased in glass at the Smithsonian because it's that inspired."

"I see. Well, just try and have a backup plan. You know, in case it doesn't sell very well and you need some change for Hostess cupcakes or something."

"You are a silly, silly woman."

No one tells you beforehand, but the funny thing about college is how it has a way of being entirely non-conducive to writing, yet highly conducive to racking up debt. Before I knew it, four years were gone, and, just as I opened my mouth to declare, "Now, I shall write my masterpiece," Sallie Mae came calling and she needed money.

I waved her off. "Not now, Sallie. I'm trying to work."

"But, you owe me money."

"I don't think you understand. I'm trying to make it as a novelist. If you need something to keep you busy, try sweeping my floor or something."

She responded by sending me bills monogrammed with my name. As a child, I could never find things with my name on them ("Paige" was very hipster for 1984), so this delighted me to no end until I saw exactly how much money I owed. I called the student loan people.

"Excuse me. Yes, um, the figure displayed on this statement seems to have a lot of zeros behind it."

"Press one to hear your balance again," the sunny voice said.

"In place of funds, would you accept some tapestries or

old incense holders I have left over from college?"

"Press one to hear your balance again."

"I guess I'll go look for a job."

Fun fact: it's extremely easy to take up a headset, get comfy behind a desk, and put your nose to the grindstone if the alternative is debtor's prison. So I did, and became very good at it. If you happened to run into me on the street around the time I was twenty-three or so, there was an excellent chance I'd regale you with tales of insurance deductibles, wood shake roofs, and insecure outbuildings. It had gotten to the point, if I ever parted ways in a friendship or relationship, the other party could expect a formally-typed non-renewal notice and a bumper sticker that said, "I'm sorry I couldn't meet your needs."

After three years, I was climbing the corporate ladder, paying my dues, eating lunch at the same table every day, and trying desperately to decide whether I wanted a tear-off or desk calendar for 2009. Ripping that page off every twenty-four hours was satisfying, but having a day-by-day as big as a baby seal sprawled across my desk, well the choice was tugging me in two different directions.

Stoically, I decided I would become the best person in insurance to ever insurance. It didn't matter that I hated every aspect of my job. I had the tiger by the tail, and that tail was insured and building a solid 401k, accruing vacation days, and possibly scoping a move to management. Management got the nice chairs and cubicle offices closed on three out of four sides. For the record, motivation usually smells like only getting caught playing solitaire thirty-percent instead of eighty-percent of the time. I was young, and if I ever got so tired I couldn't stand it anymore, I could float on to the next profession, beefed-up resume in hand.

But that was before the guy with the nice eyes and tendency to ignore the fact I snort every time I laugh shared those potatoes and a pretty impressive ring. Husband and I were married and waiting for our first herd of children. Part of me was ridiculously impressed I'd jumped straight from my plans to never get married into being able to fill a mid-sized SUV, but the other part wondered what to do next.

And so, I repeated it again and again to anyone who asked me. "I won't stay home. We can't afford it. Besides, I've worked really hard to get where I am. Why would I leave?"

My boss checked and double checked. "So, you'll be back?"

I nodded. "Of course."

"Because some moms never come back."

I set down a training manual I'd been flipping through, *So You Hate Insurance: Thirty Ways to Pretend You Like It Here.* "Well, page seven of this thing says if I tell you I enjoy answering one hundred inbound calls a day from mostly angry people because it fills the part of my soul I traded for a security badge into this place, you'll leave me alone and not try to fire me while I'm gone."

It's a well-known fact that all pregnant woman need to swear they'll be coming back to their job. It doesn't matter if they intend to or not, the accepted protocol is to never waiver in public dedication to their respective place of employment. Businesses can smell an indecisive pregnant woman a mile away and replace her with a newer, younger model before she has time to buy her first maternity support girdle. Sad, but true.

My boss looked back at me and nodded. "That's true. We're looking forward to having you back as soon as possible."

"What, and leave you guys forever? Like I said before, the badge is enough to reel me back in. You should see my picture on the front. It looks like Paris Hilton's mug shot."

"So you'll be back?"

"Absolutely."

That was that. Life decision made.

"It can't be insurance!" My bosom heaved as it usually does when I recount parts of my life drenched in utter panic yet missing ridiculous literary embellishment.

Husband stared back at me. "What do you mean, it can't be insurance?"

"I mean, I can't leave the babies. I can't. Look at them."

"They're asleep in the next room."

"Well, the next time you guys happen to run into each other, take a long look and decide whether they're better looking than a call center."

"You ok?"

We were several weeks and two hundred diapers into

maternity leave when I'd had my epiphany. Conveniently scheduled between my only bathroom break and meal of the day, nature had stopped by our quaint little home long enough to instill the type of panic akin to what a whale feels when it has overshot its lunging powers and ended up just far enough on the beach and it needs someone in a bulldozer to roll it back to the wide, blue ocean. If I hadn't had yogurt in my hair, it would've been almost poetic. Leaving my babies wasn't a question anymore. It, quite simply, wasn't happening.

I tried desperately to get my point across to Husband by using his hand to lovingly pat my face. "The children need me here. They do. I can feel it."

He nodded. "You sure it wasn't just them pooping? They make weird faces when they poop. Could mean anything."

"That too, but there was something else."

"Gas?"

The room filled with a maelstrom of emotion and an inability to articulate myself. "Do you remember that scene in *The Last of the Mohicans*? The one where the girl throws herself off the cliff?"

"You want to kill yourself? I thought you wanted to stay home."

"I do want to stay home. I meant that I want to take the plunge, throw myself into the unknown. Maybe try out a petticoat under one of my dresses. They don't seem so bad."

"But how are we going to afford it?"

The clouds parted, sun shone on my person, and I began drawing diagrams in the air with invisible dry erase markers. "It's quite simple, really. You see this part of the pie chart?"

"Where your hand is trembling neurotically in the air?"

"Exactly."

"I see it."

"That's where I quit my job."

Husband ignored my rough hewn statistics and shook his head. "You know I'd like that too, but what about the money?"

Just the question I'd been waiting for. Several weeks of pacing the house and talking to various household appliances had helped me hatch a reasonable plan. "I've crunched the numbers. Turns out, even if I go back to work, the daycare fee for twin infants is pretty much like taking out a second mortgage on the house. All things considered, if I keep working, I can pay for the cost of child care, but we'll only have a little bit of money left over."

"Great, how much is that?"

"About five dollars."

"Oh."

I patted him on the shoulder. "It's ok. I have a plan."

"And?"

"I got my degree in English, so I'll take on some tutoring work, teach five paragraph essays, encourage the proper use of the semicolon. That type of thing. It'll be great."

"Tutoring?"

"Tutoring."

He sighed. "Well, I guess that sounds reasonable. I just want you to be happy, and if this will do it, and if we can figure out the money situation, then let's go for it."

We hugged, shook on our new deal, and the next day I quit my job.

Five years, four kids, and one income later, I have yet to tutor anyone.

Chapter 2

Tightening the Old Belt

I had an interesting talk with HR the day I left work for good. As it turned out, the company would no longer be paying me. All things considered, they were very nice and broke the news to me as gently as possible.

> *Dear Mrs. Kellerman,*
>
> *Please be sure to leave the key to your file drawer on the desk and not in the actual drawer. It has been demonstrated that employees who leave their keys in the drawer have a much better chance of locking them in said drawer. We wish you the best of luck and look forward to giving the paychecks which used to be yours to someone who is not you.*
>
> *Regards,*
> *HR*

Part of me had expected I wouldn't be getting paid for work I wasn't going to do, but the reality of suddenly not having an income hit me a little harder than anticipated.

After all, I was an independent woman. I'd always paid my own way, brought home my own bacon, and overdrawn funds from an account with only my name on it. But none of that mattered now. I was home for good, and it was up to me to figure out how to stretch one income to meet the numerous needs of the household. Someone else was bringing home the bacon, and I was now responsible for frying or baking it, whatever was more monetarily conscious. Yes, I'd promised to start tutoring the minute I walked out of the lucrative door of insurance, but there were other things that needed tending to first. Before I took on any new projects, it was time to trim the fat.

In our pre-kid days, it was a given Husband and I ate pretty much every meal out or had it delivered. (If there's anything sweeter in this life than someone else cooking dinner for you, I have yet to find it.) But it was time to scrap that habit, along with other things that seemed to cost a lot of money we suddenly didn't have. With a sad resolve, I began calling all our favorite haunts.

"Hello, Renaldo's Pizza? Yes, this is Paige. Please don't look for us on Monday through Wednesday."

"Hi, Athena's Gyros? Uh huh? No, actually. I was calling to let you know we need to cancel the lamb and cucumber goodness for Thursday. The lamb will miss me? All right, tell it I'll miss it too. You don't happen to give away free sauce I can spread on crackers, do you? Never mind. Yia."

"Hola, La Mesa? It pains me to say it, but those enchiladas were my last. The Kellermans thoroughly enjoy free chips and salsa, but it'll be store bought from here on out. What? Agreed. Your chips are salted to perfection, but we're scaling back, and I've heard I can buy a can of Morton and make do. Adios. Well, wait. Do you have some type of "Free Burritos For Sad-Looking Women" program?

It took me a while to make it through the various ice cream shops, cookie dealers, and occasional seafood respites, but five hours later, I not only knew it would be a while before I tasted flounder again, but Husband's and my schedule had been cleared of any type of recreational eating. After that, I got online and started looking for other ways to save money. Surely, not eating thirty lamb sandwiches during the week wasn't the only thing we could do to make up for one less paycheck.

A day's worth of research and a drunk dial back to the Greek restaurant so I could order pitas for old time's sake later, I was able to present Husband with my findings. I nudged a notebook in front of his face. "What's this word?"

He looked up. "I can't totally make it out. Why's there salt all over the paper?"

"Never you mind."

"I'm pretty sure it says 'budget.'"

I nodded. "Yes.

I keep telling Google I stay home now, and it keeps returning this word, over and over again. What is it? Is it like one of those made-up words you try to pass off in Scrabble?"

"If we're smart, it's what we should be on."

"Right."

And back I went to my research.

"Budget." I said it out loud a few times and wasn't sure how I felt about it on my tongue. It had the consistency of taffy. The kind of taffy you find in the bottom of the barrel at an old Western store. The molasses flavor no one wants. Ten for a dollar. Sure, I'd bandied it about a few times while I was single and digging in the couch cushions for change to buy cigarettes, but it had been more in the context of, "Perhaps I should make a budget so I can afford Camels, Red Bull, crap I don't need, and my rent. No one can live like this. Ooh, there's my over-priced takeout from last night. Are you still good, takeout? I shall eat you now and go buy cigarettes."

This time around, though, I had other people who depended on me, and that fact thoroughly changed my definition of 'necessity.' My kids also looked a lot like me, which added urgency to the entire situation, the instinct never to let them sit on a street corner, holding signs saying *My Mama couldn't figure out what a budget is. Send sandwiches*, threatening to overwhelm. It's amazing really, the fact that a smaller person having the same arch in their eyebrow can spur a person on to greatness, or at least, encourage them to cut back and try to figure out what a spreadsheet is.

There had to be other ways to save money, but what were they? The student loans weren't going anywhere. I'd taken one more crack at calling Sallie Mae, and the best they offered was the chance to update my phone number so it'd be easier to track me down in the event I fled town. Somehow, closing that conversation with, "Well, it depends on what you mean by 'money,'" seemed less and less like the greatest choice of words I could've left the debt counselor with. Husband's student loans also weren't going anywhere either, the possibility the bank would let us stop paying on the car loan because we were really nice people with great hair was slim, and no one wanted to buy my hair because it'd been bleached more than a neglected lawn chair left in the sun. Nope, I needed solid, reasonable, legal ways of keeping our bank account from shrinking.

One fabulous thing I had on my side was being able to brainstorm while the twins took naps. So when the morning and afternoon breaks came my way, time became my canvas. Cigarette in hand, I stared at the clouds above my back porch and decided whether I was looking at fluffy turtles or fluffy hairless cats. The rest of the hour was dedicated to thinking up ways to hug this thing called a budget to my chest until it smelled my special blend of Calgon, baby spit-up, and the intention of putting on deodorant. After two months of sleepless nights, that stick of Dove seemed so close, yet so much work.

Admittedly, I'd definitely intended to take on tutoring students, but the never-ending, round-the-clock duties of caring for two babies at one time usually left me staring and pointing an accusing finger at the barbeque grill. "Why is this so hard? How about you start coming up with some ideas?"

"I'm not the one who said they had it under control. Maybe you could scrub pots for other people or something."

"And maybe you could cook food without lighting it on fire."

"We're all working on something."

During my internet browsing, I'd occasionally find things I truly thought could help pay the bills, and at day's end, I'd always report my findings to Husband over dinner.

"Did you know you can save a lot of money by not using water?"

He thought about it. "Like not showering?"

"Or washing dishes. Or washing anything really. I think the idea is to not use water whatsoever. I think the practice is called Non-Water Enthusiasm."

"Sounds a little shady."

"No, it sounds like savings."

"Sounds like we're not doing that."

Not washing had been a tough one to lead with, so I was more subtle when touching on my next find. "How do you feel about living in the dark?"

"Like being in a cave all the time?"

I shook my head furiously. "No, more Stevie Wonder. Or, better yet, like our gallant ancestors, the pioneers. They did it all the time."

"They also pooped outside. And I am pretty sure your relatives didn't get here until like 1920 or something."

"Which brings me to my next point."

"I'm not pooping outside."

Husband also wasn't crazy about any of the money-saving crafts I longed to throw myself into: the reusable toilet paper, the dog bowl-to-cereal bowl up-cycle, beeswax candles melted to make shampoo or tile grout…they were all shot down. The words, "Bees are fairly gentle creatures, if you raise them yourself," had barely escaped my lips when Husband got up and walked out. It wasn't until he found me buried under a stack of newspapers that he took notice of my new hobby of finding hobbies to save money.

"What are you doing?"

Slowly, I pushed a hand up through the glossy inserts and toward the light. "Extreme couponing."

"I see. Can you breathe under there?"

"It wouldn't be extreme if I could."

On that gloomy, overcast Saturday afternoon, the living room was covered from sofa to front door in newspaper ads, fliers for sales on chicken, and shreds of things that used to be blurbs for deodorant. A few cardboard keys to potential free cars littered the rug. In my quest for frugality, "couponing" had become the new buzz word, and I'd happily scooped up some old kitchen shears and tried to join the party. I'd spent an entire evening watching people on TV buy five hundred cases of Capri Sun for a dollar. One lady had been so elated at paying fifty cents for three hundred bags of dog food, she'd prostrated herself in front of the checkout and started weeping uncontrollably. Seemed like my kind of crazy train.

Husband looked at the carnage. “But you’ve never clipped a coupon in your life.”

I stabbed at an advertisement for fifty percent off quinoa. “A lot you know. Back in high school, I once clipped a coupon and forgot to use it for free mascara. When you’re young and dumb, paying full price for things makes sense. I also spent most of 1999 wearing butterfly clips in my hair. Wanna talk about that too?”

He looked doubtfully at the ad for tuna I’d moved on to and was now pushing around with the butt of my scissors. “And you think you can, uh, turn this into something worthwhile?”

“Absolutely. I saw a lady on TV drop a crate full of coupons on a cashier, and she and her husband walked out of the store with four free cart loads of Doritos. The Ranch kind. People look at you differently when you can bring home that many chips. There’s a real chance our social standing could increase exponentially. Not so much country club status, but maybe we’d get our street plowed first next winter.”

“So you’ve got a handle on the situation?”

I nodded furiously. “You just clip and pay. Clip and pay, my friend.”

I did not have a handle on the situation.

Occasionally in life, you don’t get invited to certain parties for a reason. Sometimes it’s because people know you’re the one who brings the suspicious-looking shrimp dip, and other times it’s because you always say you’ll bring something and consistently show up empty-handed. No one likes the guest who raids the cheese puffs and Coors, then floors their Ford Tempo into the sunset. I was that person at the couponing party, always empty-handed. Oh, I was well-intentioned. On Sunday, I'd grab the paper and clip what I needed. On Monday, I'd separate everything into piles, according to size and paper quality. Wednesday through Friday was reserved for admiring the piles and then rearranging them on the kitchen counter into aesthetically-pleasing flower designs. And Saturday was the day I went grocery shopping and left all the coupons at home.

One fine day, after loading my cart full of Doritos and sausage, I headed to the checkout and presented my haul, like a lioness displaying an antelope. "Look at all this stuff I got."

The cashier looked me over and began ringing things up. "Do you have any coupons?"

"Do I have any coupons?" I fanned myself with a People magazine. "My good lady, I've been clipping them and decoupaging the remnants for the past week. If I've calculated correctly, everything you see here should be free. Except this Snickers. That I didn't plan for, but life happens, and the urge to be satisfied can jump out of nowhere, like a feral bobcat."

"I see."

"So I'll take my receipt and be on my way.

"Can I see the coupons, please?"

Desperately, I flipped through my little zip wallet, felt

through my jacket pockets, and burrowed under two cases of Extreme Cheese Doritos. "I, uhh."

"Do you have coupons for any of this?"

"I must've forgotten them."

She inclined her head. "Then you owe me fifty-five dollars and ten cents."

I smiled hopefully back at her and motioned to my wallet. "Would you accept three Forever stamps and an old receipt for a car wash?"

"I'm sorry, ma'am."

"But these stamps, they never lose their value. Do you see the front? They say you can't put a price on art, but the historically accurate crack on the Liberty Bell is worth, at least, two-thousand dollars of sausage patties."

"Is plastic ok?"

"I can see you're not a fan of history."

In the almost four years I've been home, this scenario has repeated itself countless times. Cut the coupon. Forget the coupon. I'm doing my best, but until grocers start accepting my goodwill and frazzled expression as currency, the situation pretty much finds me up a creek without a dollar off beef jerky.

Despite my shoddy budgeting efforts, at the end of the day it's been the little things that have saved us quite a bit. For instance, I haven't bought new underwear since 2011. And I only bought some unmentionables that year because I got lost looking for four-for-a-dollar cookies at the Mrs. Fields and ended up at the Victoria's Secret semi-semi-semi-annual sale. I'm still a little disappointed I missed out on those tiny peanut butter cookies. Husband's made do by taking his lunch to work and accepting the fact that the "sale" pillowcase covers I found on some sort of back alley website may or may not be made out of recycled hospital shower curtains. The key is to not look very hard at the interior stitching, water spots, and *Property of Sunny Side Sanitarium* printed on the back.

Do I miss having a steady paycheck? Sure. Doing without isn't the most fun in the entire world, but it's made life a little more of an adventure.

And I love adventure.

Just don't ask me if I have a coupon for it.

Chapter 3

To Get Dressed or Not to Get Dressed

There's a timeless saying that has always spoken to me. It goes: "Teach a woman about tailored skirts, and she'll wear them when she wants to out-do others in a public setting. Teach a woman about sweatpants, and she'll laugh at your skirt and wear the same pair of pants for five days straight because they don't have a zipper."

Most things in life you can kind of prepare for. Am I great at math? No, but it didn't stop me from reading the first chapter of *Math Appreciation* in college and pulling out that C. Do I love running? Negative. But I did lie to a friend of mine, told her I liked running, and almost had a heart attack keeping up with her on the mile that might as well have been a death march. We don't keep in touch now, but the important thing is that she thinks I run, and making people think you're capable of great things is pretty much the same as actually doing them. Unfortunately, when you stay home, nothing prepares you for not having to get dressed.

Granted, I wasn't a snappy dresser when I was still working; "Homeless Chic" can be a thing, if you want it to be, but I wore pants that went with shirts and skirts that kind of went with sweaters that pilled. When the sun rose on the first day of officially being a homemaker, I knew I was in trouble, for a new age was dawning, and it wore relaxed-fit everything. During maternity leave, I'd gotten dressed to help me feel pulled together and like I wasn't getting less sleep than a meth addict, but that's because, like the freshman girl in college who thinks she'll get up at five in the morning and flat iron her hair before Physics 101, I was a rookie. On that first glorious day of being a full-time homemaker, I stood boldly and looked out the window.

"Sun?"

"Yes, Paige?"

"Today I begin a new adventure. And this adventure will be dressed in that old pub crawl shirt over there."

"Sounds good. Oh, and Paige?"

"Yes?" I said as I wiggled into my shirt with only two visible holes in it, one for each nipple.

"You may want to draw those blinds. The neighbors haven't left yet, and you're not wearing a bra."

"No bras ever," I screamed as I ran down the stairs.

Those first few weeks were unbridled freedom.

Undergarments? What undergarments?

Socks? Only if the thermostat broke.

Hair brush? Wasn't that what jockeys used to give horses shiny manes? Move over, Seabiscuit. My locks were as free as a wildlife preserve located on a wildlife preserve sheltered in a wildlife preserve. There were American bald eagles with sexier coifs than mine.

The power of never really having to get dressed is intoxicating. Simply having the option, while the sun's still up, of putting on one's pajama pants with the rip that runs from ankle to crotch is enough to ask, "Is this my real life, or is this just fantasy?" Accountability? I had none. I still don't, but in those early days, I let it go straight to my head. For the first time in my life, I was my own boss, and there wasn't a mother, teacher, or supervisor insisting I take off my stretched-out tank top and put on a cardigan so I didn't scare decent, paying customers away. I ran Braless, Inc., and there wasn't a thing anyone could do to stop it.

About the time my mane turned into dreadlocks and started singing *No Woman, No Cry* on its own, I had to check myself. Granted, I was checking all the boxes, like getting up with babies in the middle of the night, making meals while half awake, and running the vacuum for thirty minutes before I realized it wasn't plugged in, but the times where Husband didn't recognize me were also starting to stack up.

One evening, after he walked through the door, I handed Husband a baby. "You hold the lady because I have to go to the bathroom. Haven't done that yet today."

"And you are?"

"Your wife."

"Very funny. My wife doesn't have dreadlocks or wear t-shirts that say, "Ask me about my other t-shirt."

I crossed my heart. "I swear it's me. Ask me anything.

Ask me something only you and I would know."

"What's my favorite color?"

I considered. "Tiffany Blue?"

"No."

"Are you sure? It's delightful."

"Huh."

Shrugging, I flicked some cracker gunk off my shoulder. "I just really thought you'd ask me something like where we rented our first movie."

"Where was that?"

"I don't remember. I haven't slept in three months." Anticipating another inquisition, I held up an unmanicured hand. "And don't go asking me any more difficult questions, like what my parents' names are or what car I drive."

Adjusting to your first baby (or babies) is hard. Adjusting to staying home and realizing you don't have to put pants on if you don't want to is even harder. Not only are you exhausted, but there's simply no sense of urgency. You're not trying to win a beauty contest. Teenage boys checking you out are a thing of the past. He said, "Till death do us part," so if your man has problems with your skanky blue sweatpants, that's on him, right? Shouldn't he be excited to see you in the same moisture-wicking yoga pants, seven days in a row, instead of dead? Death is so permanent. Crusty wind pants can be extracted from your crack at one point or another. A spouse's gentle concern for your hygienic well-being can easily be misconstrued, especially after a new baby arrives. After a while, it's extremely easy to become a card-carrying member of the Why Is It People Even Get Dressed? club. I should know. I had mine laminated.

If, as in my case, staying home full-time becomes a reality for you, you initially become fully invested in this new club and ignore the warning signs you may be falling too far, too fast. For instance, pictures of people in clothes flood your Google searches, and characters in books seem to be wearing all manner of things laid out in flowery description, but there's still a disconnect. If you happen to have a subscription to Lands' End, the reading experience morphs from a once-innocuous inquiry into soft 100% poly/cotton blend cowl neck sweaters for winter, to one of confusion about why you just received fifty pages plastered full of kayaks, compasses, and backpackers chugging canteens full of trail mix. Had you once enjoyed compasses and nature? Surely, whoever the Lands' End people are, they realize you have no need for these "shearling pants" or "mosquito-resistant crew necks." I laughed heartily at all these suggestions, and then bought a scarf because I felt sorry for their ignorance, but also because it could be used as an emergency dish towel, a tourniquet, or to warm a small baby cow, as the picture suggested.

But, like I said before, Husband had started getting a little concerned about me wearing hospital pants seven days a week, when the closest I'd ever been to becoming a doctor was the time I'd screamed and put a band aid on a chocolate bar that fell out of the freezer prematurely and cracked in half. "Code brown" actually means something delicious around the Kellerman residence.

While I only advocate getting dressed on a daily basis if you work outside the home or if you're the type of person who likes to wear things that match on the regular, I have spent the last three years crafting a "uniform" of sorts to suit my housewifery. And by "uniform," I mean guidelines. And by "guidelines," I mean ways to not terrify people that may or may not drop by unexpectedly during the day. Over time, I've deduced that halfway dressing oneself can really help with morale and the smidgeon of purpose needed to power through another twenty-four hours. I'm not talking about full tights and sweater sets, here. Again, just trying not to horrify.

Uniform Guidelines

Wear a bra: It's extremely important that this is done at least three percent of the time. One percent is dedicated to times when the trash must be wheeled to the curb. Another percent is designated for the times you're only wearing a button down and need to tell the kids to stop talking to the strangers considering buying the house next door. The last percent is reserved for speaking to solicitors who didn't buy the fact that, when they knocked, you told all the kids to get down on the floor, be extremely quiet, and pretend they're reenacting the tunnel evacuation from *The Great Escape.* By the way, the dog sold you out and barked his head off. He doesn't care because he doesn't wear a bra.

Put on a shirt: Or don't. Sometimes it's the only way to get rid of solicitors the dog didn't.

Any shirt will do. Old college tees, tank tops, that billowy number you save for when the Renaissance Festival rolls through town, all are acceptable. My only stipulation is to aim for something that's not see through or something that flaps open of its own accord. Sometimes the only way I've been able to tell if the shirt I'm wearing is covering enough is to quiz the next-door neighbors on how much or little they know about my birthmark. "It's not a swan," I insist emphatically, and run to burn certain tube tops or makeshift bandeaus.

Wear something on your bottom half: I find this is the area I'm most lax in, but it's usually the most important. If it were up to me, I'd only wear pants one percent of the time. Pants are cumbersome and remind my muffin top just where it stands, or rather, hangs in life. Not only that, study after study shows pants are the leading cause of car or house keys poking you in the crotch if you sit down too fast. Unfortunately, society feels it would be happier if I muffled the sound my thighs make when they slap together. But seeing as that sound is remarkably close to David Bowie and Mick Jagger's remake of "Dancin' In the Street," I can't really hold a grudge.

Now I'm not saying you have to wear pants all the time. Underwear works for about thirty-eight percent of most days, but the rest of the time, life interjects and says,

"Hey, the mail's here. Don't you want to see if that used copy of *Quilting For People Who Can't Cut Straight Lines* you bought off Amazon made it? Not to mention that case of cookies you threw in your cart at checkout because of Super Saver shipping?" I usually nod and acquiesce to the fact I must cover my lower regions so the neighbors don't start knocking my trashcans over and leaving old swim trunks on my front porch. Not only that, children tend to bike through here, and I just wouldn't be able to live with the thought they peddled away thinking they'd just spotted one of those pants-less meth addicts their parents warned them about. This is especially likely in my case because I'm usually muttering something about bleach, Robitussin, and the children trying to light things on fire.

There's a little leeway here. Depending on the day, I may gravitate towards different things that hide my faded Hanes Her Ways. Pants are well and good, but oversized nylon shorts, sarongs, and curtains with a well-placed belt will all get the job done. If I have to go somewhere in public, I simply make sure to remove any leftover tassels from the curtain. All I'm saying is don't panic and start screaming, "Where'd I put my St. John's Bay cargos?" when you clearly have options.

As strenuous as my standard uniform regulations are, I've been overjoyed by the rise of this century's greatest fashion achievement. I can't really have an honest conversation about modern housewifery apparel without giving a nod to my now-close friend, yoga pants. Not since the vest has a garment transitioned so smoothly from day to night, weekday to weekend, and sleeping in to giving a Nobel peace prize acceptance speech. There's really nothing yoga pants can't do. I once asked a pair to parallel park my car, and they just nodded and said, "Yeah, ok."

I've found there's no stronger staple in my daily clothing arsenal than black yoga pants. Some people emphatically disagree with this idea, based solely on the objection that yoga pants are "lazy," "slovenly," or, my personal favorite, "not fit for audience with either the Pope or the President." Quite frankly, I look forward to proving that last one wrong, papal audience pending. To the dissenters I must ask, how can I not throw sincere adulation at a garment that doesn't require actually attending a yoga class, but also allows me to throw on some heels, a jacket, and bowtie, and hit up a swanky dinner on a second's notice? Or, at the very least, patrons of that same party would accept I was there to serve hors d'oeuvres and peach sangria. I don't know about anyone else, but when I see a waitress in yoga pants, I tip her large sums because she's efficient, and also because there's an excellent chance she'll own that restaurant one day. Yoga pants are the pants of dreaming big and dreaming comfortably.

Husband's made peace with my yoga pants and even appreciates how I'm able to coordinate them with a pink t-shirt for lounging during our downtime together, and with a yellow t-shirt when I surprise him at work. Now that I think about it, though, I haven't seen the blue hospital pants in quite some time. Perhaps he's finally come to terms with my perpetual pants without zippers due to the fact he made my thrift-store scrubs come to terms with the bottom of a local landfill.

I once heard something extremely profound on an episode of the animated series *Spiderman.* "With great power comes great responsibility." That was a full year ago, but I still can't help taking those words to heart. My days at home are still my own, but the passage of time has pushed me past being completely disheveled all of the time, directly into being disheveled only part of the time. Attempting to avoid being perceived as a drug addict, needing to go to the grocery store, and trying to set the example for my children that pants should be seen in a positive light—all of these reasons have banded together in a sort of support group of reasons to propel me into getting fully dressed some days. The simple act of putting on an actual outfit can make me feel I can take on the world. It really does. Fortunately, most days, I have absolutely no urge for world domination. However, on days I desperately need a pick-me-up, I go ahead and cram my butt into some cute jeans and put on makeup. You won't ever find me vacuuming in high heels, but I can put on blush and open a can of tuna with the best of them. Those days excluded, I live in the comfort of my uniform. After all, there's no shame in starting the morning by proclaiming to the sun shining bright through my window, "No bras, forever."

Chapter 4

I'm Just a Girl, Standing in Front of a Mixer, Asking It to be a Paperweight

Whether it was because I forgot to add the yeast or because I dropped the entire bowl of dough on the ground, the Easter I ruined the dinner rolls is gone—but not forgotten. The creation of the rolls was a sacred tradition entrusted to me, and I, like none of my hardworking and culinary-skilled ancestors before me, turned what should've been sumptuous pieces of lightly-floured heaven into small rocks suitable for propping up lawn flamingos or chucking at ponds situated on the front of Hallmark cards the world over.

This particular incident happened in 1998. I know this because my mother is quick to tell the story whenever I mention any impending foray into cooking, baking, or shellacking bread. And although she strongly maintains it was due to some profound dumbassery my sister and I were committing instead of paying attention to the rising dough, she's always quick to add that, at the end of the day, I'm actually a decent cook. This would be sweet if it wasn't horribly wrong. Bless the woman. Jesus should let her in to heaven based on this ambivalent perception of me alone.

The fact of the matter is I'm an atrocious cook. Absolutely terrible. Actually, if I've ever accidentally poisoned anyone reading this book, please accept my deepest apologies and know that when I read "flounder" in *The Joy of Cooking*, I thought it said "flambé," and since I had no idea what flambé meant either, things got out of hand.

When Husband and I were dating, I was able to cover my inability in the kitchen by happily suggesting places which would make, plate, and sell food to both of us. There was nothing more romantic, I posited, than having a complete stranger roast our chickens and garnish our glasses of ice tea with small wedges of lemon. On most of these occasions, I'd wait for a lull in conversation, take a moment to shake the bread basket and quietly declare it "bread I might think about baking."

"What?" Husband asked one evening.

I set the bread back down. "What?"

"You just whispered something about baking while I had my head turned."

The power of suggestion is a complex thing. I needed Husband to subconsciously think I could slap a loaf of rye into shape, but I didn't want to have to *prove* it. We were still engaged. This particular Achilles heel could wait for its grand reveal after we walked down the aisle. Looking back down at my plate, I shrugged. "You must be hearing things."

"But I could swear you said you were thinking about baking bread."

I turned my attention back to ferrying the noodles around on my plate before I answered. "Nope, sure didn't."

There were a few token times I did try my hand at cooking dinner for Husband, mainly because I heard significant others put more confidence in their mates if they knew they could boil water on their own. Luckily, I was able to avoid serving most of these ugly Julia step-Childs to my love by coming up with handy excuses such as:

"When I went to drain it, I dropped all the pasta we were going to eat down the sink."

"I know I said we were having pork chops tonight, but the people at the grocery store said pig was very last season and they refuse to carry it."

"Fish? No, I'm not making salmon on Friday night. I meant I was fishing for compliments. How does this dress look? Be careful how you answer. Empire waist looks best on me, and this is a wrap dress."

Shortly after I quit my job and waved goodbye to the long list of restaurants and carryout establishments we'd dutifully patronized, the realization that I was now responsible for crafting meals in the kitchen dawned, and a special sort of panic set in. After all, it was only logical. I calculated the data on old takeout menus. Husband would be working from sun up to sun down, and, if the family wanted to eat before seven o'clock at night, someone needed to fire up the frying pan. Or the oven. Or possibly the hot plate. I still wasn't sure about the most reliable method of culinary preparation. Luckily, right at that moment, an old fortune from a fortune cookie slipped out of the takeout menu I'd been scribbling on and fell into my lap. It said, *You are that someone. Lucky Numbers: 1,2,3,4,5. Try our chicken!*

The only thing I was completely sure of in this whole mess was the essential task of hunting and gathering. From here on out, food would not appear on the doorstep, no matter how long I waited next to the front window and pawed at it. Grocery shopping was about to become my business. Was there anything worse? Plowing through crowds of people, price checking, trying to figure out whether a gallon of milk was overkill in the event that a half gallon was inadequate...I'd been watching my mom do it for years and never envied her for a second. The rare times I'd grocery shopped in college had consisted of throwing two cases of shrimp-flavored ramen in the basket and sprinting out the automatic doors so fast my knees had hit me in the chest. At least those had been solo trips. Now, I not only had to make a list and start stocking the cabinets, but I had two babies to take with me. I needed to figure out how to get the twins in a grocery cart along with everything I intended to buy. Two children who couldn't walk or carry anything left precious little room to tote around bread, milk, and Advil.

The morning of the first trip dawned, and I did my best to first muster courage, and second, rally the troops.

"You, floundering on your stomach, you're in the Baby Bjorn. You over there, trying to put your fist in your mouth, you're in the front of the cart. Well, let's not sit around staring at each other. We've got canned corn to buy." Figuring out how to grocery shop with twins had never actually made it on my life's to-do list, but there we were, one baby in the cart, one strapped to the front of me in a carrier. The simple act of having kids makes you realize you're capable of things you never thought possible, and then it requires that you do them or die trying. I looked like an overwhelmed camel with its hump on the front, but there wasn't an alternative. It was either that or starvation, and the camel was hungry.

A note to all my new moms out there. Shopping with kids is harder than trying to style your hair the way the stylist did it the day before. Not impossible, but frustrating, and there's a little more skill involved than you'd originally anticipated. It takes years of practice to execute a remotely smooth trip, and, even then, the whole thing looks like a train wreck from the outside. Ask any woman with grown kids whether she ever managed to nail down shopping for produce while having any sort of meaningful conversation with her toddler, and she'll simply start laughing hysterically. No one told me this, which is why I spent my first few jaunts to the local supermarket dancing to Phil Collins on the overhead speakers, trying to get the babies to laugh, and throwing random items in the cart in between high kicks. "Easy lover! Watch out, kid, baked beans comin' your way.

Duck. Shh, don't cry. Momma's never applied her interpretive dancing to this particular song. Be patient, and maybe they'll play 'Land of Confusion.'" The sheer feat of trying to entertain the twins while remembering where the lettuce was was maddening.

An added bonus, I found out, was all the free commentary I got when I ventured out to gather food during the day:

"You sure have your hands full."

"A boy *and* a girl huh? It must be nice having identical twins."

"Sure I can help you find the detergent. Did you know you have a lot of babies?"

The consequence of a thousand distractions, I returned to the homestead laden with all sorts of odds and ends I was sure could be combined into meals, but this common-sense wisdom was called into question once I went to whip something up for the dinner hour. Sure, I'd made a list, but singing "Mary Had a Little Lamb" and trying to remember to buy actual lamb turned out to be impossible. The good news was, we'd made it out of the grocery store without losing anybody, I'd only cried three times, and all the groceries had been transported from car to kitchen, using minimal swear words and a solitary "shit" as I fell backwards down the stairs with a three-pound tub of butter.

Just as big a question as shopping for the food was what to do with two babies while I threw something together. One child in a roll-y seat, another swinging from the doorway in a Johnny Jump Up, and me poking my head in the cabinets, trying to take inventory of what we'd triumphantly returned with ultimately produced some complicated plans of action. Not only was I now required to start mixing the random things I'd found at the store into a meal, I also had to entertain my offspring while said mixing occurred. Fun Fact: This is one of the reasons I hate cooking and will as long as I have small children. Perhaps I'm a horrible person for saying that, but cooking around little ones is just plain hard. And by "hard," I mean "a horrendously torturous experience." Oh, all I have to do is stir the mix thirty times, pour it in a pre-floured pan, and whip the egg whites for the meringue, all while standing on my head? Hold on, let me just make a bottle, break up a fight, and pull the toddler out of the toilet first, and I'll get right on that. This recipe calls for little bits of toilet water, correct?

The odds and ends were never very promising. "Well, we could dump these baked beans into the strawberry yogurt, but I'm not sure about the taste or the laxative effect. Could be like shooting a fifth of Mylanta. Who suggested the spaghetti noodles? Because we forgot to get sauce when we had to stop and do a diaper change, but it looks like there's a stray can of clam chowder we could drop some red food coloring in and try to act casual when your dad gets home. Hmm, no ketchup to speak of, but a corndog dipped in tartar sauce might pass. I'll just have to sell it while adopting the misplaced optimism of the doomed and the drunk."

Most people only get one surprise birthday party in their life. But very few people get a surprise dinner made of mystery ingredients every night for a whole year. Husband was one of the lucky few. It wasn't until a particularly shady meal of creamed corn and croutons that he whispered, in grave tones, that we'd received what he'd thought was a cookbook for a wedding gift. He was unsure if what he'd seen was me propping up an uneven table with half a set of his/hers encyclopedias or something with a casserole on the front.

I was insulted. How was I supposed to build ships in a bottle—if I ever took up building ships in a bottle—on an uneven table? Then again, could we go on eating meals that had crackers as the only course? With how distracted I'd been at the grocery store, things were fast getting out of hand. I glanced back at my soul mate. The aggressive way he was drowning a crouton in a river of runny corn spoke of both urgency and despair.

I inclined my head. "You're right."

"About what?"

"Planning. I need to plan some meals. Get organized before I head out to the grocery store with the kids. I can't promise I'll use a cookbook, but I'll talk to the internet and see what we come up with."

Husband nodded so hard he looked like a bobble head doll. "There's probably a ton of stuff out there. And I'll eat whatever it is you decide to make. I just don't like fresh tomatoes, stewed tomatoes, mushrooms, cream of mushroom, black olives, pizza with more than two meats on it, pizza with a crust thicker than one centimeter, shredded chicken, lettuce that isn't Romaine, ham, sausage gravy, any kind of dessert besides cheesecake, and most grains."

I got up and started rooting around for the cookbook. "That's it, huh? I think I speak for everyone when I say we're all excited you survived infancy."

In its essence, meal planning is a siren song of ease and relaxation, the efficiency of it all reeling the planner in with words like "simple," "bulk," and "an idiot can do it." The reality of meal planning, however, is that it turns into a game of How Few Ingredients Does It Take to Make a Meal? Or the culinary game of chicken I like to play, called Three Ingredients or Bust. If a recipe calls for four ingredients, I immediately break out in hives and abandon ship. Don't worry though, the internet has you (and me) covered. There are approximately eight hundred million websites containing recipes, meal plans, people who'll plan your meals for you, and a blog run by a woman who doesn't meal plan but will let you and your family come camp on her organic farm for six-hundred dollars overnight and promises not to stare at you while you sleep. To say I was overwhelmed with choices is an understatement. Did you know there are seven hundred ways one can prepare salmon? I wasn't aware letting things cook in the dishwasher was even an option. I am now, and now spend most of my time jealous of people who have cleaner fish than ours.

For a week, I hunted down meal plans suited to my

skill level. Unfortunately, just as it seemed I'd found a carefully mapped-out itinerary of biscuits and chili, one meal would go and jack up the rest of my plotting. This continues to be the case today, mainly due to the fact I'm lazy, and also because it's unfair to post six days worth of corndogs, grilled cheese, and beef sliders only to throw in *brazed duck with the head attached, surrounded by a bed of greens picked from a moonlit field at midnight. Suggested sides: carrots grown with exactly eight sections, olives picked fresh from the tree growing next to the Temple of Athena, and cottage cheese made from the milk of precocious and well-read goats who love anything by Charles Dickens.*

I made it through *David Copperfield*, but that didn't mean I knew anything about brazing meat. What I do know is that meal planning works for some, but was making me feel completely overwhelmed. This was the case right up until the day I heeded Husband's first suggestion and started seriously looking at our cookbooks. Originally, I'd laughed at the idea of cracking open one of those intimidating tomes, usually emblazoned with a smiling-yet-homicidal-looking spoon on the front, but as I sat on the back porch one afternoon and peered through a haze of cigarette smoke into the kitchen window, I couldn't help thinking the stack of cooking geniuses the world over thrown to the back of the counter might just have something. I also thought if I could simply flick the butt of my Camel the proper way, there was a chance I could incapacitate a squirrel and dinner would take care of itself.

Naptime only half over, I had thirty minutes to wander back inside and shuffle through all the various books we'd received for wedding and shower gifts. Before I knew it, I was elbow-deep in pink bindings and paragraphs describing how to sauté beef that had already been sautéed so it no longer tasted sautéed but as if it had been roasted on a bed of chestnuts in an open glen. Sauces, glazes, plucking a duck before it realized it'd been plucked, recipes I could tell had spirit, jumped out and desperately tried to walk me through the twenty-eight simple steps to making my own gourmet chocolate ganache. And, just as I stumbled on how to properly use a candy thermometer to either make Peppermint Divinity or test the level of motor oil in most compact cars, I saw it.

I winked. "Hey there, good lookin'. What's your name?"

The book with the tan cover and modest illustration of a silver pot sauntered over. *Quick and Easy Crockpot Meals.*

The chemistry sparked between us like a pair of improperly placed jumper cables. "Quick and easy? I like that."

"You're about to love me."

I giggled nervously. "Why don't we take this to the couch?" I lugged my new friend over to the loveseat and burrowed into my favorite corner. The sun was lustrous as it danced over the pages, delicate print chock full of ingredients and only one small phrase of direction. *Place everything in the pot.*

"Book?"

"Yes, Mam?

My heart raced. "So, what you say here is that I only need to dump all the ingredients in the crockpot and turn it on?"

"That's right."

There had to be a catch. "But what are the rules, provisos, quid pro quos?"

"Do you quote *Aladdin* to all your cookbooks?"

"The ones that intrigue me."

"It should be a hoot working for you, lady. Yes, all you have to do is toss everything in, turn the dial, and forget about it. By the way, you may want to throw the other cookbooks away. It's cruel to lead them on. You're with me now, and I'm pretty sure *Better Homes and Gardens* cries herself to sleep at night."

For the next twenty minutes, *Quick and Easy Crockpot Meals* enraptured me with practically instant macaroni, in-a-snap hot cocoa, and cinnamon rolls made by the closest thing to magic I'd ever come across. Not since the first time I saw *The Labyrinth* had I been so drawn in by the ethereal, or dare I say, enchanted by it. There was almost nothing the Crockpot couldn't do. Page seven did state I couldn't ask it to drive me home when I was drunk, but I had Husband for that. I'd never made bread, but page twenty-seven said it wasn't a problem. A little yeast on a low setting yielded eight dozen French baguettes. Page thirty-two vouched for the fact I didn't even need hands: if I could pour a bag of frozen vegetables and two cans of beef broth in with my teeth, a passable stir fry could be accomplished.

Elated, I promised to henceforth dedicate my home life to the Crockpot. There was simply the small matter of finding it in the dark abyss I'd banished it to after the wedding. Later that afternoon, the twins were privy to watching me dig through the cabinets, extracting my new best friend, the confusion on their faces apparent when I hugged the appliance instead of drawing circles in its dust, like I frequently did the Kitchen Aid mixer. I brandished the silver and black treasure in front of my small companions. "This, my friends, will be our salvation. For soon its recesses will hold shredded chicken, effortless puddings, and possibly, if I don't get too lazy to buy all the ingredients, monkey bread. What say the counsel?" I took the gurgles of one fat baby and the passing out of the other as affirmation, and began preparations for what would surely be Husband's new delight and joy.

The next morning, cream of chicken in hand, I filled the miracle machine with Campbell's cream of chicken soup, a packet of seasoning, chicken breasts, and a block of cream cheese. Lovingly, I gazed at the yellow and white blob sitting atop the raw meat. "You're beautiful. I hope you know that." Carefully, I set the glass lid back on top of the Crockpot, turned the dial to "low," and called across the counter. "Hey, *Quick and Easy Crockpot Recipes*?"

"Yes?"

"How long do I cook this for?"

"Four to six hours."

"You sure? That's pretty much the whole day."

"Look out, world, the lady gets my appeal."

"No need to be a smart ass."

"Enjoy your chicken."

For the rest of the day, I did laundry, played with the twins, made a sandwich, stared at the wall across from the toilet, checked my email, contemplated whether certain compliments I'd received in college had been backhanded or not, almost bought a two-year supply of Bare Minerals, took up crocheting, quit crocheting, changed diapers, and explained to my little boy and girl how important a good education is, but not to rule out community college or an excellent vocational school right away. Plumbing would always be a respectable profession in the Kellerman house.

I did anything but cook.

Around five thirty, Husband tromped up the steps and into the kitchen. I gestured widely with the metal ladle I'd procured for my goings on. "Darling. Come gaze upon what I've made you. There's witchery in this pot, and methinks you'll love it."

He looked skeptically at the steam making its way out of the Crockpot, engulfing the face I was now hanging over it. "What is it?"

"Dinner."

"What kind of dinner?"

"Chicken I left unattended all day. Seriously. I poked it once at two o'clock, but it was pretty much left up to its own devices."

"I see."

I motioned to the cabinets. "Let me make you a plate, so you may sample the product of a true modern marvel. And to imagine I once thought of turning this magnificent machine into a planter."

Hesitantly, Husband took the plate and shoveled a fork-full in his mouth. "It's good," he mumbled through pasta and chicken.

One of my proudest days will always be the one the twins made it screaming into the world, but the twenty-four hours in which I made my first edible something from the Crockpot also brews strong feelings of pride within me. In a way, I'd birthed something beautiful. And it needed to be turned down to low because it was searing to the bottom of the crock.

Beaming, I dished some out for myself, and was pleasantly surprised Husband hadn't been lying. Not that he's a liar; he was simply treading on delicate ground. "Mmm."

"What are you doing?"

"Savoring the fact what was simmering in here all day didn't turn out to be hot tar."

He dug his fork back into his plate. "It is pretty good. I wouldn't mind eating it again."

I considered. "Would five days a week be too much?"

From that moment on, I was a devoted follower of the Crockpot. To this day, I salivate over the word when it smacks me in the face during my internet meal searches. Put that whole pigeon on low for eight hours? Done. Throw brown sugar, evaporated milk and an expired box of pudding in there, cook it overnight and enjoy homemade grape jelly the next day? Love to. Husband's taken to my choice method of cooking, and, despite the fact I once made him purple soup, he seems to go along with my insistence that I can cook anything in the Crockpot. Heck, I'd be up for shoving a Honda Civic in there, if I could just find the right recipe. Occasionally, I'll catch my lover looking longingly at the stove, probably with dreams of a nice honey baked ham in mind.

But, as long as I'm a housewife, the Crockpot shall be my trusty steed, the lid, my shield, and a ladle as my sword. "Onward to meal planning," I'll cry.

Just don't ask me to make rolls in it.

Some things in life simply aren't feasible for me. Easter or not.

Chapter 5

Breaking News: Pinterest Threatens to Make Drinkers (or worse drinkers) of Homemakers Everywhere.

The first year of my housewifery was spent in peace. I don't mean the type of peace where nothing was lit on fire or I didn't almost accidentally maybe sort of poison Husband with some questionable salmon, but the type of contentment where I was blissfully unaware there were other women doing a much better job at pretty much everything I'd perceived myself to be mediocre at.

The night I discovered Pinterest, the ice in my highball tinkled against the glass and rung out the music of quitting time. Children in bed and Husband yelling at *Halo* somewhere, my trusty gin and tonic and I leisurely perused the interwebs, reading articles of high import, things like whether the Loch Ness Monster had, in fact, been spotted outside the Loch, swimming somewhere around Lake Ontario. And just as I declared to no one in particular, "Probably, because those fins imply a fantastic long-distance swimmer," a link caught my eye. I dropped another teaspoon of tonic water into my gin and decided to plunge down the rabbit hole. "Hmm, the thumbnail says it has something to do with a black sweater I may or may not want. Ok, I'm game. I love black sweaters shrouded in mystery."

With a twitch of my right pointer finger, I was deposited on a red-lettered page. I looked at the dog, who was now staring up at me from the living room rug. "Pinterest. What's a Pinterest?"

He rolled his eyes and went back to stalking a piece of cookie camped out under the coffee table.

I mulled it over. "Pinterest. Pretty sure a friend of mine had to have one of those lanced once. Sounded painful." Still, I couldn't confirm this because the page claimed I had to be "invited" to join the community. The black sweater was nowhere to be found, but my interest was piqued. I was obviously on the outside of some clique, looking in. But to what? What was I being excluded from?

Probably a black sweater.

Did I really need to know?

Yes.

No.

Yes. The black sweater was now my white rabbit.

I refilled my glass and went in search of someone who would issue me an invite. After being accepted and setting up the obligatory account, I stepped into the middle of something I didn't have the ability to comprehend. That, or I might've had too much gin by that point. Actually, I was sure of it. Five minutes prior, I'd yelled at the dog, "Another drink for the lady."

Images of clothing, witty quotes, and assorted pictures of celebrities clung to the screen in virtual bulletin board format. I'd had a bulletin board in college. I stuck concert passes to it and notes that made no sense, sometimes pictures of people in Halloween costumes I barely knew. This was different. Well, there were also pictures of people in Halloween costumes on here, but the captions weren't "Such a fun night! Thanks for helping bathe the neighbor's pet emu in Sam Adams! XOXO."

After some navigation, I realized Pinterest was a place where people of a certain age could share and hoard collections of things they like. "Ooooh, I get it! Pinterest. Interest. I have interests!" I liked things. I was also boring and had no idea if the general public went out after 10:00 p.m. anymore or if they ate less than a gallon of cottage cheese a week, so I began to get to know the site. It didn't take long before it dawned on me this was a place people such as myself also shared recipes, cleaning tips, and pictures of Mark Walhberg with quotes from *To Kill a Mockingbird* overlapping his face.

Elated, I began dividing half my free time between staring into space and "pinning" things to my virtual pin boards. I had a board for shoes, another for clothes I would only look good in if I were a twenty-one-year-old Russian model with an eating disorder, and one titled "Things For My Imaginary Lake House." One night, just as I was about to add thirty new mascaras to my board "Puttin' My Face On So I Don't Scare People," I caught a glance of what some other people in the community were adding:

Decorating Tips For Spaces That Are Already Decorated Better Than Your Living Room

Meals Made From Ingredients Found At Grocery Stores You Don't Live By

Fun Games To Play with Children Who Can't Lift Objects Yet

How To Build Barn Doors to Look Like Bedroom Doors You'll Then Use As Doors To Spruce Up Your Old Barn

The feelings of inadequacy were immediate and acute. It seemed there were other homebodies who were putting in real effort, thousands of women beautifying their homes and interacting with their children using hand-sewn ABC quilts. Just that afternoon, I'd counted three new cracks in the wall and noted a stain that looked like a body, seeping up from the carpet padding in the linen closet. The children were almost always in mismatched outfits, and the closest I'd come to educating them on anything was to put both twins in a wicker basket full of books and watch them laugh hysterically and try to climb out. Someone would always tip the basket over, and all three of us would guffaw as babies rolled across the living room like marbles. Anne Sullivan, I was not.

The new, overwhelming sense that I was a failed homemaker began niggling at me day and night. At breakfast one morning, I decided to step up the game and start fixing my many flaws. "Do you think we need a new headboard?"

Husband put his coffee down and gave me a confused look. "But we just bought a new bed while you were pregnant. It came with a headboard.

I glanced down at my computer screen full of inspiration. I'd been busily pinning things and drinking coffee out of cups I was sure The Pioneer Woman would've confused with ash trays. "Yes, but did you know there are people out in the world crafty enough to make their own headboards?" I lamented.

"Out of what?"

"I'm glad you asked. And thank you for your interest because I've got one right here we can throw together using things we have around the house. We simply need to make the initial investment of an upholstery gun, two yards of main sail from a ship that's been to sea at least twice, and some twine. But I think we may have twine in the garage somewhere, so strike that last one."

Husband reunited with his coffee. "That's crazy."

I paused my Amazon search for utility knives and raised an eyebrow. "The only thing that's crazy is we're the only people on earth without a quilted headboard and matching side table lamps crafted from raffia and up-cycled copper stolen from our neighbor's air conditioning unit. Pinterest says so. Damn it, man, we're suburbanites. It's time we start acting like it."

"What's Pinterest?"

"Only the foremost authority on how we should be living. And on that same note, I'm sorry I haven't hung any pictures up since we moved in."

"I'm not sure I'm following exactly what you're talking about, but you should probably leave the bed alone."

"I guess so. But is that a 'yes' to turning all of our wedding pictures into a collage? Apparently, we've really been slacking. Two whole years in this place, and not so much as a family vacation frame over the toilet. If we don't have some kind of gallery wall parading up the stairs in the next month, we're technically supposed to register as Appalachian hill folk."

For a brief moment, I became a woman obsessed with finding ways to make my home just like everyone else's. How had I been so blind to the fact most people have heated bathroom floors, trellises strong enough for climbing into all rooms of a house from the outside, and monogrammed refrigerator doors? They say ignorance is bliss, but in my case, ignorance had caused my children to miss out on diapers with their names stenciled on them with ink made from dried plums and henna. Would they grow up cherishing their childhoods or, instead, contribute a chapter, respectively, to a memoir, entitled, *Where Was My In-Ground Pool?*

My poor children. After quite a bit of thought and hesitation, I sat them down, each with a cracker, and had the talk. Damage control needed to be done early.

"You're probably wondering why I've gathered you here in one spot when, clearly, nap time just ended. First of all, I'd like to make it abundantly clear this is not a second morning nap time. There's been some talk about this happening, but I say a lot of things."

"Ma?"

"I do have more cookies, but it'll have to wait until after the meeting."

My little boy drooled on himself, a clear sign he'd already noticed his lack of privilege. "Ball."

"Any complaints about lost toys should be directed to Human Resources. Your father will be home at six. Now then, it's come to my attention there are parents in this world who dress their children in matching outfits and shoes with more than eighty percent of the tread attached upon purchase. Right now, this isn't a problem because you haven't been walking long, but when the day comes you lose that game of tag by falling on your face abruptly, I'll have no choice but to feel guilty."

They seemed to be taking it ok. Someone chewing on their foot queued me to the next topic.

"So, while I'm apologizing for your clothes bought on consignment, I'd like to jump on the opportunity to throw out a mea culpa for not carving your initials in your cribs, hand-painting a jungle mural in the nursery, or ....what?

"Baa."

"Well, Pinterest said to call it a nursery. Apparently, 'that room where we keep the children' isn't as classy as I thought it was."

For the next few minutes, I tried my best to go over the specifics of why I'd never pinstriped the twins' walls or made them building blocks from dough made from my tears, salt, and flour. I finished with a flourish and an offering of more cookies. "But all is not lost, my small ones. Your mother is going to start crafting things. Oh yes. Things that will make you say, 'Wow, you're the best mom ever.'"

One baby knocked the other one over.

"Good enough."

My spirit more than willing, it was simply a small matter of follow through. By quick estimation, there were roughly seventy-three projects I could do to improve our quality of living, and I was ready to see them all to completion. That is to say, I'd do them at some point or another. Crafts and I have a complicated relationship. As projects to beautify one's home, they require a certain amount of elbow grease and commitment to fulfill one's dream of a *Better Homes and Gardens* life, mostly via glue gun. One has to put in the blood, sweat, and tears. The name of the game is effort, and in return, the reward of being able to boast to guests, "Yes, it took forever to find the right vintage anchor to refinish and hang over the fireplace, but it was so worth it."

I, on the other hand, am lazy and broke.

For instance, on Monday, I set my sights on re-doing the entryway, building matching cubbies for everyone in the family, and adding crown molding to every room. However, after realizing I'd need a circular saw, something called a miter box, and a way to haul two kids and sixteen pounds of plywood back in a Chevy Blazer, I ditched the day's plans and watched a marathon of *Monk* instead. Our shoes would forever be thrown in a haphazard pile, but I had to hand it to Tony Shalhoub for tugging at the heartstrings and also challenging the way most of us approach a puzzle and/or seeming paradox of the criminal variety.

Tuesday, I decided on a fresh start and fired up the old computer to find and purchase a new zebra-print rug for the master bedroom. Pinterest promised it would be chic. My bank account promised we wouldn't eat for a month. I turned off the computer, made a sandwich, and decided, until we won the Powerball jackpot, drawing a smiley face on the stain that looked like a giraffe in far right corner of my room would have to pass for sufficient whimsy and elegance.

On Wednesday, I had to choose between taking the babies to the doctor or replacing the fixtures in the bathroom. Both were all-day projects, but should I buy everything I needed for those hanging, mason jar pendant lamps or thunk down the cash for a copay? The kids could possibly fight off Scarlet Fever, but the right lighting would make me look five years younger. At the time of this writing, I've made peace with the white, plastic monstrosities that dangle above me in the water closet. Thursday wasn't much better. I took one glimpse at the list of supplies for "How To Make Placemats Out of Twigs" and remembered I had to do laundry or send Husband to work in some of my yoga pants. Though cost effective, I had to push my stick-gathering plans back to Friday.

The last weekday smiled through my window and I hid under the comforter. The twins had been up all night, and

I had no intention of picking up twigs or switching gears to the project I'd originally scheduled for Friday, putting together and painting a papier-mâché canoe to mount over the dining room table. In a haze of exhaustion, I threw a pillow at Husband's back, while he was getting ready for work, and shouted, "Make your own damn canoe," before falling back asleep.

By the time the weekend rolled around, I had exactly zero projects done. No glass-front cabinetry installed. No suitcases made into side tables. There were people in this great world who could field covering everything in canvas and moss in a non-ironic fashion, but I simply wasn't one of them. Even though I felt the twinge of defeat, something in the back of my brain ended up telling me this was ok. Husband would've told me the same thing, but I think he was too afraid I was eight seconds from making him a headboard out of leftover wine corks and hand-stamped quotes from less-than-successful Nicholas Cage films. Did I really need to strive for perfection in order to be a homemaker? Probably not. Would my kids hold it against me that I'd dropped the ball on making them their own toy boxes out of reclaimed Balsa wood? Maybe. I'd decided to stay home to be with them. Hopefully they'd look back and remember all the crappy kids' movies we'd watched together and not dwell too hard on why we never gave them their own Jack and Jill bathroom with heated floors.

Besides helping me come to terms with the fact the rooms in my home will always be covered in toys and not rattan baskets filled with firewood, Pinterest forced me to shake hands with mediocrity. The Sunday that ended the week of failed projects mediated the conversation between mediocrity and myself. Between sips of Folgers and bites of frosted donut, I leveled with this new ally.

"Mediocrity," I said. "My name is Paige. My floors are always dirty, I don't have a Christmas tree for every room in my house, and my kids may have only bathed once last week."

"You eat donuts this late in the evening?" he asked.

"Yes, Mediocrity, I do."

"We're going to be great friends. Better even than Courtney Cox and Jennifer Aniston."

"Probably. As long as I don't have to be in shape like either one of them."

"Paige, I'm king of the mundane, not a treadmill."

I inclined my head and then looked up. "Would you like a donut?"

"Sure, but if I drop crumbs on the floor, make sure not to sweep them up until tomorrow."

"Deal."

These days, with gin glass in hand, I still peruse Pinterest, but I stay away from anything that requires me to shatter glass with a small hammer and mosaic my kitchen floor. I can barely keep up with laundry, let alone find out where the cool moms are buying tiny hammers these days. However, I hold a deep love for searching for clothes I'll never buy and shoes appropriate only for the times I'm accidentally hired as a runway model in Milan.

Oh, and pictures of Robert Downey, Jr. overlaid with quotes like, "People Who Love Gin Live the Longest." You don't have to be perfect to stay home, but it helps to pat yourself on the back, once in a while, and love the space you already have.

Chapter 6

The New Ikea Catalog Says Placing the Kitchen Sink By a Window Makes Doing Dishes More Fun. It's Also a Good Reminder of the Futility of Escape.

John Donne once said that no man is an island. But John Donne wasn't a housewife. Wikipedia tells me he was a lawyer. I'd argue housewifery turned me into an island, or the island's second cousin, Woman Who Talks to Herself More Than the Average Person Talks Themselves. When it comes to staying home fulltime, I've heard a lot of differing opinions on what makes it difficult. Some say it's the massive amount of time spent with one's children. Others vouch no person should be required to walk by the refrigerator and notice it's leaking for the two-hundredth time that day. I, on the other hand, maintain "Little House on the Prairie Syndrome."

The first time I noticed the isolation, the shock was so immense, I forfeited the heated debate I was having with myself about whether vanilla pudding really had the edge over caramel, and stood perfectly still. Or maybe I was sitting in front of the pudding cabinet. Regardless, it was the silence that first caught my attention. Well, it wasn't complete silence. "Love's Theme" was playing on the laptop, but that was the terrifying part. There were no other adults around to physically stop me from listening to disco. Slowly, I started to recall how, four hours earlier, I'd also tried to do the splits in my bedroom during a particularly energetic interpretation of "Stayin' Alive." No boss had stopped by to tell me to cease what I was doing and head to HR. No neighbors had knocked on the door because they heard a giant pair of pajama pants rip.

In fact, no one had called at all. In days.

A wave of panic washed over me, along with the need to confirm I was still surrounded by adult life forms. Timidly, I padded over to the other side of the master bedroom, stuck a screw driver in the storm window, pried it up, pushed the screen out with my foot, and delicately stuck my head out. "Hello?"

A squirrel threw an acorn at my forehead and went back into a tree I'd never seen before.

"Anyone out here?" I yelled. The wind whistled through the yard and tousled the spaghetti sauce in my hair. Last night's dinner had been delicious, but I still hadn't had a shower since the day before the last seven days. This horrified me as I gazed across the acorn-littered yard and caught a hint of movement across the fence diagonal to our house. Could they see the sauce? No, the slightly hunched over old woman who shuffled out onto her cracked patio didn't seem to notice me. I watched her light a cigarette and stare into the yard. From what I could tell, the woman with the Marlboro was the only sign of life anywhere. Every other house around us was silent, every yard empty. She suddenly looked directly at me and blew a casual ring of smoke, denoting her comfort with being home in the middle of the day or possibly some sort of disdain for the bed of violets directly in front of the patio. I, on the other hand, chewed on the spaghetti sauce and slid back in the window.

Kansas had been settled quite some time ago, but it suddenly felt as abandoned as the early prairies. Husband was going to need to get home early so he could help me churn the butter and tend the smokehouse. And I hadn't even budgeted for a smokehouse. We'd have to make it through the winter purely on our own gumption and canned goods. In shock, my back found the bed. "I don't even know how to can." I pointed at the dog. "Well, you're here. Do you know how to can anything?"

He rolled his eyes and walked out.

"I bet the Wild West wasn't settled by even one boxer," I shouted. "If even one of your great great great cousins had caught a deer, I'd be shocked." Ugh. I was even talking to the dog too much.

The silence closed back in, and how many ways excessive solace could sneak up and make itself known to a person paraded across the popcorn ceiling. My pointer finger traced the imaginary list. "Huh. Who would've thought number seven would be 'Spends too much time staring at mediocre-yet-cost-effective ceiling coverings'?" Not 1975, that's for sure.

At dinner, I broached the subject with Husband. "Talk

to me."

He stopped poking dubiously at what was in the Crockpot. "Talk to you? I just said hi when I walked in the door."

"Mmm, your voice is delicious." I cooed.

"What?"

"Maybe not as delicious as the chicken I have cooking in there."

"I'm not sure what I'm supposed to be talking about. That's chicken?"

"It's chicken."

We stared at each other for a few seconds before I wagged a finger at him. "You stopped talking."

Husband backed towards the doorway. "I'm gonna go take a shower now. You sure everything's ok?"

I nodded. "Yes."

"Good."

"No."

"You're lying to me?"

"Nope."

"Then why are you hanging onto my ankle?"

I tried to act casual. "Thought your shoelace was untied. A wife's first duty is to make sure her husband doesn't fall down the stairs in some sort of one-foot-in-front-of-the-other disaster scenario. The second is telling him she doesn't mind watching *Casino*."

"I'd believe you, if you weren't holding onto both my ankles now. How can you not like *Casino*?"

"I love it. Oh look at that, chicken's ready."

My first attempt at talking to my love about the day's isolation wasn't a raving success, so, after the twins went to bed, I plopped down next to him on the couch and proceeded to stare at the side of his head. "Hi."

Channels rolled by on the cable guide, and slowly Husband's eyes slid to the side before he said, "Hello. Can I help you?"

"Talk to me."

"Ok. Would you prefer to watch pro wrestling or the history channel? There's absolutely nothing on."

"Oooor, we could tell each other about the minutia of our days and then read way too deeply into every conversation you had at work. You start. Wait, I'll start. I think the way that guy talked to you was ridiculous, and his pants are hideous."

"I have no idea where you're going with this, but everyone I work with wears the same type of pants."

Ignoring his lack of enthusiasm, I proceeded to fill Husband in on the day's observations, pointing out the deafening lack of adult voices and the Marlboro Woman. Besides the twins, she'd been my only confirmed sign of life anywhere in the vicinity, and the prospect of hurtling three fences to shake her hand, only to be told she actually smokes Virginia Slims and needed to get back inside to watch her stories was too much to handle. "So, we just smoke and stare at each other during nap time."

Husband flipped past *Dateline* and settled on a shark documentary. "But I thought the twins were keeping you pretty busy. I don't talk to anyone at work either."

Oh, where to start? The task in front of me was like trying to sell the joys of Spanx, door to door, in a nudist colony. "Yes, but you have the option."

"The option to what?"

"Talk. You know, 'Hey, Bill. We never got your fantasy football money.' And then Bill's all, 'That's because my grandma died and we all pitched in for the cedar coffin she wanted.' And then you stare back because you feel terrible, and let him go on his way. You know, small talk."

Husband shuddered. "I hate small talk. You know that. But what I'm really hearing is that you're lonely. Maybe you should find some friends who stay home too."

Men. Why are they always trying to fix things, when all we want is for them to agree with everything we're saying and then go buy beer and chocolate to share? I threw my hands in the air and swatted away his words. "I don't want your reason and rational right now, thank you very much. It's so like you, thinking you can just stroll in here with your hair doing that thing that made me want to marry you, and then throwing around ideas that make sense. You, sir, are out of line."

He shook his head and turned back to observe the feeding habits of Arctic Great Whites. "I'm not entirely sure what you're upset about, but that's just my suggestion. What about my hair?"

Breath puffed out my nostrils. "Don't worry about it. It's just unnatural for someone to have perfect, slightly tousled bed head all the time. It's magical, and I hate the power it has over me. You're like a really distracting, sensible unicorn. If you're going to look wind-swept and sensational, I'd rather it be when we're discussing something that's not so important. Like cheese."

"Finding people to hang out with would probably be a good idea. Or maybe finding a hobby."

"I'll do you one better.

"Oh, what's that?"

"I'll do what any self-respecting castaway would do, and start a journal. That way, if I ever disappear, someone can find and send it to a museum."

"Why would you disappear?"

"People die suddenly all the time."

"I hope not. You're responsible for the children."

"We'll simply agree to disagree."

"About being responsible for the children?"

"About the journal."

He breathed a sigh of relief. "Good. I think. And if you do decide to take my advice about making friends, don't lead with anything about unicorns."

The next day, after Marlboro Woman and I wordlessly observed each other for the time it took my Camel to burn down to the filter, I sat down and got started on my journal.

December 1, 2011
Dear Traveler,

You've found the journal of one Captain Paige

Kellerman, commander of our modest abode, master of no particular talents except juggling different-sized objects as an ice breaker at parties. As they say, who needs a nametag when you can toss several staplers in the air at one time? We've been adrift in this modest suburban home for several months now. Very few signs of life. Although, I'd be hasty excluding the neighbor's two dachshunds, which go out of their way to sneak across the street and back to sniff me while I'm getting the mail. The longer I'm stranded, the easier it gets to imagine them as a backup food source. Kind of like Ball Park wieners, but different. At this moment, I eat yogurt and talk to myself the majority of the time, so the dogs are safe, for now.

The two first mates are decent company. Once they learn how to talk, things should improve exponentially. Right now, they solve their conflicts by slapping each other over things like who gets to be called First Mate, which is why I have two of them and no bosun.

When I'm not cooking, cleaning, or watching the Today Show, my free time is spent on the deck, filling the bird feeder and waiting for rogue squirrels to stop by and steal all the food I just put out. As far as I can tell, the squirrels seem to be the greatest threat to the local bird population, which must be starving, while the squirrels probably have no pants that fit. I'll try to rough out some sketches for documentation. Note to self: Send Husband into town for some pencils and Crayola watercolor paints.

To the person who finds this journal, please forgive me for hiding it under the bathroom sink. It's the spot mostly likely to be overlooked when we do the yearly cleaning of the bathroom. All I ask is you tell the world we were here, afloat in our eerily quiet neighborhood, not so much living off the land as killing it with dog poop, and making faces at each other to pass the time. I'm aware you're reading this probably hundreds of years in the future, but, for historical reference, on a scale of Donner Party to Lewis and Clarke, we've found ourselves mostly at a Captain James Cook.

All the Best,
Paige Kellerman

While I'm not sure anyone will ever find that note hastily scrawled on the back of the third Little Debbie box I'd emptied that week, the lack of adult conversation and uncomfortable staring contests with the woman across the lawn eventually gave way to an unexpected hobby besides useless journal entries. I'd already tried all the expected pastimes of a house-bound woman for five seconds and thrown them to the curb: cross stitching, hand dipping candles, scrapbooking by staring at the scrapbooking supplies in the craft section at the store and going to get a two-pound bag of Twizzlers instead. Dead ends. That's not to say many of those things aren't fantastic, they simply weren't my cup of tea.

The day I found it, I hurtled two kids, the dog, and the KitchenAid mixer to tell Husband about it.

"I found something."

He looked me over. "Whatever the opposite of sleeping pills is?"

"People."

"People? Where? Do you need me to tell the door-to-door pest control salesman to go away, again?"

"On the internet. They want to be friends with me."

He gave me a knowing look. "Honey, most of those people are from Russia and want our credit card."

Excitedly, I danced a jig while I shook my head, managing all at once to look like someone they test experimental shock therapy on. "No, it's called blogging. I write things and then people talk to me."

"They do?"

"Yes. The people in the computer are my friends."

"And they told you this, Carol Anne?"

"They have no choice. Anyone who interacts with me, I automatically label them as 'friend,' whether they're aware of it or not. If you send someone a Christmas card and they've never technically seen you in real life, is that too forward?"

Slowly, he shook his head. "Forward? I think the word

you're searching for is 'illegal.'"

Triumphant, I pulled an old roll of holiday address labels from the junk drawer. "The thing is, you told me I needed to make friends, but I actually kind of hate leaving the house, because, as we all know, that requires putting on pants."

The look on his face was doubtful. "Or any clothes. Is that a t-shirt or a tablecloth with a hole in it?"

"I'll have you know, faux silk robes with tattered tank tops underneath are all the rage at Paris fashion week right now. Listen, I understand how it sounds, but you also have to understand I've found a way to contact the outside world without needing to wash my face first."

And, just like that, a blog was born, the sunshine of adult interaction emerging from the clouds once again. It was free. It connected me to outside life. When I posted something, no one knew the horrible state of the spaghetti sauce in my hair. (Heck, one of my new readers had disclosed that she, too, had found leftover food in her bangs.) Glorious. Sure, I wasn't exactly mingling with people in person, but I was finally able to get all the thoughts that jumbled up in my mind all day out into the world, and, afterwards, get feedback from other friends and parents that I wasn't alone. We weren't cavorting around the town fountain or lumbering across the lawn to borrow cups of sugar from each other, but sharing stories of solidarity and laughing together on the little website I'd put together, and on the various other social media outlets available, about the day-to-day drag of life was refreshing.

From that historic moment on, I've only had to talk to myself fifty percent of the time. It's how I managed to kick isolation in the butt and not let it get its hooks in me. If you happen to find yourself in the same position, don't ever let anyone tell you computer friends aren't real. The loneliness of staying home is a real struggle. Over the last five years, I've forged some of the best relationships I've ever had with people I've only had the pleasure of meeting once or twice. You never have to feel like an island. Do what works for you. In my case, Husband is just glad I don't spend so much time staring at the side of his head and asking for the intimate details regarding what kind of pants everyone wore to work that day.

Oh, and on a follow up note, just this year, I spoke to the lady across the lawn for the very first time. She was very sweet when she told me she wanted to finally say 'hi' and to tell me we had snakes in the space between our yards. Sometimes it's better to pretend you're trapped in isolation.

Chapter 7

Bills, Bills, Bills

I have a few collections I'm truly proud of. The pictures I've remembered to take of the children, a few essays written in grade school and college, and assorted socks without matches all make me smile wistfully, but it's the ever-growing pile of "balance due" notices that really gets my motor running. White ones, green ones, ones that live under the refrigerator, they all get the special welcome speech before they're shoved into the bill rack on the counter. It goes something like, "At least you're not red. Have a nice day."

Before you assume we don't pay our bills, let me make it perfectly clear, we do, it's just we'd rather set fire to them, and use the whole kit and caboodle to heat the house so we can dodge the gas company this winter. Those people mean business. They also may be pirates or have incontinence problems. I haven't decided which. We're like any other family, however, and there's only so much money to go around. And, like most other families, it comes down to someone to budget that money and remember to mail the check, enter the credit card number online, or send the carrier pigeon with a sign around its neck, saying, "If received, please wait for a second bird carrying mostly not hot checks."

Before I decided to stay home, the bill paying was split down the middle, a scenario which can be summed up thusly:

"I thought you paid that."

"You said you were going to send that."

"No, I clearly remember hearing you saying you dropped it in the mail."

"Then you clearly remember wrong."

"Maybe I clearly remember you didn't remember it last month."

"Well, I guess we'll just give the car back to the bank."

"I'm going to make a grilled cheese sandwich."

In that particular conversation, making something to eat wasn't pertinent, but it was an excellent way to move to the kitchen so I didn't have to admit that perhaps I'd forgotten to send the payment in question. Also, I love grilled cheese at almost any point in the day, except when I'm in the shower. The whole thing was frustrating, but at least we had the luxury of always thinking the other party had dropped the ball. Marriage, we're super good at it.

Six months into being a homemaker, and without even realizing it, I'd started stalking the mailman. (I'm not sure he recognized it, or ever has, but over the last four years, I've become an expert at staring at people through my blinds and flipping them shut before the subject in question gets suspicious.) Three-thirty in the afternoon was accompanied by the promise of catalogs, value mailers, coupons I wouldn't use, and bills. My day usually had two or three high points, and getting to sift through random crap sent by people who didn't care about me usually came in solid at second place, the first forever being morning coffee. This sounds a little sad, but you show me someone who doesn't like pulling out an unknown stack from their mailbox, and I'll show you someone who hates suspense.

Every day, I threw out the useless ads for diet pills, pocketed the keys for cars I'd won, and, finally, sorted the bills into the bill rack on the kitchen counter. In the middle, things that needed to be paid, paid invoices shoved on the bottom, bobby pins and nail clippers on the top shelf. Figuring I had a little more time than Husband to see to one of life's most annoying duties, at the beginning of each week, I went through the rack, grabbed the most urgent notices and took care of things more or less on their due date. Day upon day of this extremely technical system, and time eventually handed over the task of "Bill Payer" to me, in its entirety, and asked that I not screw it up. Or maybe it was Husband.

"And you're sure you want to take over paying all the bills?"

"Sure do."

"It's a lot to keep track of for one person."

"I've been doing it anyway."

"I guess so. But you do forget things sometimes. Remember the beta fish?"

"You killed the beta."

"Have at it."

In the game of housewifery, this particular phenomenon seems to present itself more than any other. A quick definition:

In Charge of Everything
Verb

The act of becoming the one responsible for everything having to do with running a house, by the pure circumstance of being the only individual at home all day.
The act of forgetting to shower.
i.e., She drinks a lot because she's in charge of everything.
See also: howls at the moon, drools from corner of mouth, and quit smoking but thinks about picking it up again, hourly

So, it fell to me, but it wasn't all bad. For instance, one of the huge perks around managing a family's finances is experiencing the comfortable feeling of seeing the balance in the bank account and desperately trying to match it up to that month's much larger stack of bills. What makes this moment special for me is how I get to keep it for my very own, like a locket, or one of those *best friends* heart necklaces that has two halves, but I have both halves. Ok, maybe I've exaggerated a little bit. Sometimes I'm not completely by myself. Just yesterday, I picked up the electric bill and waved it at the entire family. "This is what happens when no one turns off the lights after they go to the bathroom. New mandate: everyone poops in the dark."

Another upside to controlling the import/export of payments is pretending that everything was exported on time. At the end of the day, when that late notice rolls in, you only have yourself to fight with.

"I thought you sent the student loan payment, Paige."

"Um, I thought so too, but, apparently, there was a marathon of *Psych* on that day, and I forgot. It'll be our secret."

"Sounds good."

Don't get me wrong, it's nice to be able to haggle over whose fault it is with your significant other, but, when you're the only one in charge, at least the rest of the partnership doesn't have to know how close you came to losing the house.

You're also the only one who knows that perhaps the cable bill due on the twenty-first of November might not need to be paid until the first of December. The stretchery of funds has fallen to you, and if things are a teensy bit late, so as not to overdraw the account, well, so be it. Taking complete control of the finances afforded me the opportunity to practice the newfound skill of finding new days for things to be due on. Not too far in the future, of course, but when it comes to student loans, well, Wednesday's basically the same as Saturday. I happen to be fluent in "Grace Period," and have used the last five years to perfect the dialect.

Husband passed the bill paying on to me just in time

for him to never become acquainted with exactly how many days of leeway we have to pay for things. This leads to me having to reassure him, from time to time. For instance, he stumbled on a stray cable bill I'd stupidly left out, hoping it would pay for itself. "Is this a double bill?" he asked. "Looks like there's been some sort of overcharge."

I shook my head. "Not to worry, we have two days."

"You mean we owe all this still?"

"Technically, yes. However, we still have two days to pay the prior balance due, before any of the late fees really kick in. After that, we have an additional month until the current balance due is actually due. If we didn't pay that by the current due date, we'd be up a creek, but because I'm paying the past due balance tomorrow, it will catch us up until next week, and we're back in good graces again. It's simple, really."

"And you're sure that's how it works?"

"They haven't shut off the cable yet."

It wouldn't be such a juggling act if the billing departments of these various companies didn't show their generosity by making sure they send out payment notices that are all due on the same exact day. No one talks about it, but there's no doubt in my mind there's a board meeting held every year, and the electric, gas, loan, mortgage, and magazine subscription divisions of the world hold a quick vote.

"All in favor of having every bill due on the fifteenth of every month, say aye."

"Aye."

"All opposed?"

"Put your hand down, Collections. We know you have sneak attack privileges, so stop rubbing it in."

I've become an expert at making sure the mortgage, credit card, and car payment all get paid in the same week. From the fourteenth to the twenty-first, the rest of the family has become accustomed to eating Teddy Grahams and applesauce. Plans for new underwear also keep being pushed farther and farther into the future. Like I tell Husband, "Good things come to those who wait until they're seventy-five."

It's almost shocking how many bills it takes to run a household. Even more delightful is how many things you can be charged for. One particular afternoon, between eating peanut butter out of the jar with my hand and waiting for the dryer's siren song, I scanned the water bill and then looked down at the twins busily breaking the childproof locks on the cabinet containing the toaster and a stack of napkins. "Ok, which one of you was it?"

"Mama?"

I waggled the paper in their direction. "Says here there's a fee for treating the water. Who here isn't happy with the quality of the water?"

"Wanna cookie."

"First you don't like the water, and now you want a cookie? What's next, a mint on your pillow?"

A little research illuminated the fact the city treats the water here so we don't all get dysentery. Still, I'd become hyperaware of the most minute charges on every bill, and now I had the time to critique them, a skill I put to good use the day we received the itemized billing for the third baby's birth. I scanned the three, crisp pages, about had a heart attack, then stopped in order to prevent additional hospitalization and a five-dollar charge for three or more bed pans. Carefully, I examined the list:

Taking baby out

Wrapping baby

Making sure baby made it to correct mother

Choosing shortest route by gurney back to hospital room

Every supply in room

Removal of dignity during catheter extraction

Allowing only visitors bearing gifts of food into room

Admittedly, that last one had been my request, I simply didn't realize there'd be a surcharge. At any rate, the total amounted to the same as purchasing an adult elephant to carry me out to get the mail. I rang up the billing department of the hospital, determined to say my piece and ask why I'd been charged for thirty Diet Cokes, when twenty-nine was a little closer to the mark. Staying home all day has hidden perks, like getting to spend hours on the phone with people who like you for the money they think you have.

Ring Ring

Operator: If you're calling because we overcharged you, press one. If you're calling because we undercharged you, press two. If you're calling because you feel the amount of bed pans listed on your invoice is incorrect, press three.

"Hello, this is Sally in billing. How many bed pans can I put you down for?"

"Hi, Sally, this is Paige Kellerman. I actually picked your extension because I wasn't sure where to go. Oh, and before we get started, is number two on the menu an actual option?"

"Thank you for contacting us, Mrs. Kellerman. Yes, it is, but due to lack in usage, that operator is now the vending machine stocker."

"I see. Well, the reason I'm calling is I received my bill for my post-partum stay, and the amount is pretty large. Is there any way we can break it down into payments?"

"Are you sure we didn't add extra bed pans?"

"Yes. Well, there was a fee for not walking in on me in the bathroom, but that seems legit…I think. Thing is, we're on one income now, and splitting the bill up would be a lot easier than selling one of the children."

"Are you sure? Perhaps you like the new one better than one of the old ones?"

"Unfortunately, we love all of them. Is there anything you can do?"

"Hmm, we can break everything down by twelve."

Breathing a sigh of relief, I leaned against the counter. "Fantastic. Twelve hundred years would really help us out."

"Twelve months."

"As in 'Thirty days has September,' type months?"

"The hospital requires all balances to be paid within a

year."

"Sally?"

"Yes?"

"We were charged for five thousand bed pans I didn't use."

Twelve months later, we made our last payment to the hospital. I celebrated by waiting until the mailman stopped looking at the blinds, then running to the mailbox for my value mailers. We were finally free from the shackles of medical billing. It had been hard, but the struggle was over, and we officially owned our third child. Much wine would be consumed this night. I creaked the rusty door open and felt around for our own, special pile of useless advertisements, but, instead of coupons for free burritos and queso, inside the little metal box was a new invoice.

Dear Paige,

A year ago, our billing department fell into disarray and forgot to send out enormous bills our clients owed us for hospital services. Please pay the following $374.00 for services rendered to your child.

Love,

Your Pediatrician

I trotted back inside and stuck that one in the middle of the bill rack. Thank goodness it wasn't red yet. I think we have until two days before our fourth baby arrives to get the balance due paid.

Five years in, and I have my system pretty much down. Sometimes, people ask me if I hate being the one who's in charge of the administrative side of the household, and admittedly, it can be a little daunting sometimes. Bills eventually gave way to also filing all the taxes, knowing where all the important paperwork is stored, and being the only person who knows how to order extra birth certificates, social security cards, and two-hundred begrudging dollars in rabies vaccinations for an ungrateful cat. On the flip side, my inner control freak has flourished, and I'd be hard pressed, now, to relinquish my hold on due dates and debit cards. I guess what I'm saying is, if you're looking for someone to do unqualified CPA work, I'm your girl.

I may even send you a receipt by carrier pigeon.

Chapter 8

Everyone Can Just Go Naked

Have you ever truly smelled a dryer sheet? I mean, really smelled it? Delicious. Then again, that could be the dryer sheets talking. Spend enough time in the laundry room, and weird habits start to develop.

What?

Yes, I'm well aware laundry is a universal issue. People from all walks of life put up with the hassle of tumble drying, pre-treating, and testing to find out if that smear is dirt, chocolate, or poop before the garment in question is balled up and thrown into the watery abyss. It's not something reserved for those who stay home all day. The Dirty Scourge has been following me since the days of my youth, when my mom pointed to the basement and said, "Don't drop that by my feet. No time like the present to learn how much you're going to despise losing socks for the rest of your life."

Nope, laundry has always been a constant in my life, but it wasn't until I committed to the twenty-four seven of watching the home front that it became a full day's annoyance. And, for the first time in my two-and-a-half decades of life, I realized I didn't simply dislike laundry—I wanted to run it over with my van. Then back over it. After that, drive toward the closest nudist colony and enroll. Shortly after said enrollment (depending whether there was a welcome packet I needed to go through), I'd drive around until I found the laundry pile, and run over it again.

In the beginning, our relationship was fairly civil. Every morning I walked past the pile next to my door and nodded politely. "Laundry."

He'd always kept to himself, so it never surprised me when I received a brusque, "Paige," before he looked back down at the ground. While I was working and out of the house all day, this morning interaction always struck me as quaint and something I didn't necessarily carry with me to my lunches at Chipotle with co-workers. But something started happening, day after day, week after week of walking the halls and rooms of our house. It seemed to suggest the laundry was replicating.

One afternoon, just as I was exiting the twins' room, I noticed a pile of dirty socks and miniature jeans staring back at me from behind the door. Puzzled, I pulled at a rogue chin hair. "Laundry, is that you?"

"It is."

"But I just saw you in my room."

"Yep, that was me too."

"The pile under the couch? Arm chair? The stairs down to the basement?

"I get around."

Shrugging, I turned to go. "Well, decent people don't sneak up on other people. Try to stay in one place. Or, at the very least, clear your throat so I know you're there, mmmkay?"

"You're the boss. I'm just here to make your house smell terrible."

For the rest of the week, things didn't get any better. It felt like laundry was everywhere, popping out when I was at my most vulnerable. Dirty rags by the sink, shirts on the counter, an unexplainable pair of underwear in the oven drawer. I finally had to confide in a friend.

"It's like everywhere I go, he's there."

She sympathized. "Have you told anyone about what's going on?"

I shook my head. "No, just you. It's only, I'm really scared now. I was in the bathroom this morning, counting how many seconds it would take the kids to find me and start asking questions like, "Why are you hiding from us?" when there he was, hiding under the cabinet next to the trashcan."

She wrapped her arms around herself. "That's horrible. I think I've seen that guy. Acts like a towel that got dropped on the ground, but when you pick him up off the ground, there's like ten pairs of boxers and a shoe under there."

I looked her in the eye. "That's the guy. What can I do?"

She looked down at her booted feet, which had suddenly become fascinating. "There's nothing you can do. Cops said they have no jurisdiction until he makes a move. And, wouldn't you know it, he just lies there."

He did lie there, and he did accumulate. However, unlike that one day of second-grade dodge ball, I refused to be the victim. I was home all day. He'd be in every room, and I had no choice to look at him, but that didn't mean I couldn't hatch a plan of attack. Growing up, I'd watch my mom whisk away the laundry, drag it to the basement, and sort it into meticulous piles of whites, darks, sort of darks, kind of whites and underwear she preferred not to touch with a ten-foot pole. She ran a smooth assembly line, thousands of pounds of other people's clothing, rinsed, pre-treated, soaked, and then thrown in the machine. After which, all garments were either hung on the drying rack or thrown in the dryer. There was a brief time where everything was hung out on the clothesline, but after a few years that was discontinued. Part of me feels this decision was due to the time I found a roach in a pair of purple biking shorts, screamed, and stripped down in front of the neighbors, but no one can say for sure.

Roaches aside, I was ready to translate the efficiency of my mother into some sort of equally well-functioning system involving bleach, resolve, and a bottle of actual Resolve.

Author's Note: A recent interview revealed my mom had the laundry down to an art due, largely, to the fact she used the rest of the time hide from us and read things that interested her. When asked for a quote, she responded with, "Why are you going through the pantry? You don't live here anymore." And now, back to the story.

It would be a little bold of me to call what I do to the laundry every day a "system," but there isn't really a more civilized word for it, and "screams at shorts and throws them down the stairs," doesn't exactly trip off the tongue. I've found the only way to cope with the piles that confront me in every room of the house is to buy color-coded laundry baskets and train everyone in the house to use them infallibly.

Kidding.

While those strategies may work for other people on the planet, every Kellerman in this house has resigned themselves to intentionally throwing their socks three inches short of said basket, tub, or trough with a "Throw Underwear Here" sign attached to it. One day, anticipating Husband's itch to take off his socks, I stood up, wrapped flashing Christmas lights around my head, grabbed a box, and yelled, "Hey, throw that dirty laundry in this designated receptacle." He threw them over my head and behind the sofa. Before the twins were born, I waddled out to the store, bought the cutest hamper of wooden burlap construction you ever did see, and placed it, triumphantly, in their clean, color-coordinated room. Eighteen months later, I walked in to find they'd broken it into pieces, used half the pile to construct what I estimated to be a future tiny bonfire for roasting miniature marshmallows, and used the rest to build a ladder to escape out the window at a later date. A pile of miniature socks was later recovered from the heat vent under the far right crib.

I'm also guilty of tossing yoga pants and t-shirts on the bedroom floor more often than I'd care to admit. Granted, my track record is ten times better than anyone else under this roof, but, sometimes, the urge to simply toss my bra on the closet floor gets the best of me. Therefore, the way in which soiled garments are now regulated is somewhat of a necessity for all of us. It's all very technical, but in the interest of helping my fellow man, I'll share my secrets, just this once. Pay attention, or you might miss the half-assedness of the entire thing.

The Ten Point Laundry Attack

1). Get up in the morning. If you're not awake, you can't do laundry. Or, you can go back to sleep. When you're asleep, laundry doesn't matter. This is actually a solid choice. Start again tomorrow. No one ever died from wearing the same underwear two or three days in a row, except perhaps the early settlers, and that was probably a lack of quality soap. How clean can boxers get, if all you're using is lard?

2). Walk the house and assess the size of the laundry situation. Walk from room to room, kicking each pile you find. Make sure it's not a pet or child before you really let loose. Sometimes, the dog looks like four-week-old fitted sheets, and I have to stop myself before it's too late.

3). Pick one pile to wash. That's right, only one. Don't be a hero. Trying to do all the wash in one day is a catastrophic choice that leads to over-exertion, frustration, and, in my case, stomping around the backyard with no pants on out of sheer protest. The cops have only had to come out once, but, as it turns out, if you yell, "I'm trying to Shout it out," enough times, they just leave you alone.

4). Drag your chosen pile to the laundry room. If that particular room happens to be on a lower level, do as I do, and kick it down the stairs. If you're lucky enough to have a wash room on the same floor, throwing it against the wall and telling it you were lying when you said it looked great in pleather leggings is equally effective. This is a perfect time to get creative with your insults and use all those vocabulary words you've never had a chance to employ. Go ahead, call it a sycophant, or try to work "triumvirate of power" in there. It deserves it.

5). Tell the kids you're off to do laundry and that they should stay put for a few minutes. Listen as they follow you down the stairs.

6). Spend the next fifteen minutes pulling children out of the washing machine due to an overabundance of "help."

7). Stuff in unsorted clothing and start washing machine.

8). Stop machine and extract child who managed to crawl back in.

9). Clean out dryer lint trap.

10). Debate whether to go back upstairs or make a fake beard out of the just-harvested lint. You think about this for a while, but decide against it. Husband would appreciate the comedic complexities of the whole thing, but the time it would take to find duct tape and wood glue seems draining.

If repeated, faithfully, every day, this simple system should get you done with the week's laundry just in time to start a new week's laundry. And, just to confirm, no, I don't sort things into piles of respective colors. For this reason, my mom's whites are still really white, whereas, guests in my home usually get to play a couple complementary games of "Is This Towel Dirty or Chartreuse?" Don't worry, if you happen to find yourself in my bathroom, wondering about that precise thing, I make up for any emotional trauma by handing out free, slightly pink socks.

I wish I could say staying home all day has given me an edge on the never-ending cycle that is washing, watching the children dress themselves in five different outfits, and washing everything over again, but I'd be lying. Truth be told, I once tried to throw everything in a garbage bag, haul it down to the river, and scour it against an old-timey washboard, primarily in the hope the river would wash it away and whoever found it would spend the rest of their day wondering whether the twelve people who'd lost their pants had sent out any other clues to their whereabouts. The washboard was promptly up cycled to a sign, which I staked out in the front yard, advertizing all of our clothes were for sale.

At the end of the day, Husband doesn't really mind if I'm super on top of keeping up with the laundry, as long as I'm not doing weird things with the various cleaning products we use. Namely, when the more mundane aspects of retrieving socks from the lint trap set in and I want to spice things up, I'm not allowed to make my own detergent out of things I have lying around the house. Homemade detergents are all the rage right now, and I've been itching to jump on the soap-grating train, but my other half, fearing for the safety of the resident machine, his supply of pants, and the house in general, has put his foot down. He also hid anything that could be used as a grater. Actually, the laundry's pretty lucky to have Husband around. Everyone needs a friend in a high place, and, if weren't for my better half stepping in, here and there, to do some loads of work clothes, I would've set fire to the entire production some time ago.

One evening, Husband barely prevented what would've been a delicious-smelling crime scene. I'd just bent over my victim, when my love's horrified voice called out from behind me. "What are you doing?"

I didn't look up. "Doing what I should've done a long time ago."

"Why are you rubbing dryer sheets all over a stack of dirty boxers?"

"I'm smothering him."

"I see."

"You don't understand. All day, everywhere I turn, he's there, sitting smelly and contemptible. I went to sit down and eat a PB&J today because I thought I'd killed him. Nope. He jumped right back up."

The air went still while Husband knit his brow. "What was it? A sock?"

"Old dish towel. Smelled like mildew and paprika."

"We don't even own paprika, do we?"

"Exactly."

As he ripped the dryer sheet from my hand, Husband gave a comforting nod and shoved me towards the stairs. "Why don't you take a break, and I'll get it from here."

By the time you read this book, I still won't have a good hold on how to keep the laundry from stalking innocent people, but rest easy knowing I fight the good fight every day. Which is why I'll be dropping the admission forms to the nudist colony in the mail tomorrow.

Chapter 9

I'd Like to See Someone In HR About the Benefits Package

For the fifth night in a row, my shift had run late. Clattering pans in the sink, I wondered whether I'd missed the quitting bell, or if my boss had gotten drunk, passed out, and forgotten to send me home again. About the time I whacked the last of the cooked cheese off the baking sheet and stuck my head outside to see if the neon sign said "open" or "closed," I remembered I was doing dishes in my kitchen and I was self-employed.

As I poured old wine in to a day-old glass, I couldn't help thinking the late nights were killing me. The dishes were almost done, but I still had to do laundry, pick up toys, and figure out why the cat was licking the window screen outside the living room again. His mental problems on top of pulling Mega Blocks from under a couch Calista Flockhart couldn't fit under left me wondering whether I'd looked over my employee orientation packet very well. Maybe I'd been too excited to have my picture taken for the name badge. Or had it been the new, bra-less uniform that had distracted me from going over the company benefits with a fine-tooth comb?

My back found the front of the stove, currently encrusted with old clam chowder and oyster cracker crumbs, and, while I slowly sipped my five-dollar wine, I couldn't help thinking I should've had a beer instead. But, besides that, it began to occur to me that I needed to find someone in HR to explain exactly what the benefits of my new position were. One thing was for sure, perks didn't come in the form of not cleaning clam chowder off stove tops. The stuff behind me growled a couple times before I smacked it with a wash cloth and went in search of answers. I found Husband in the next room.

"Hi."

"Hello."

I smoothed the hem of my t-shirt and plopped down next to him. "We need to talk."

"Yes?" he asked.

The sweat from my brown dripped on the arm of the couch. "It's this new job. I'm still unclear about what my hours are."

He shrugged. "They're what you want them to be. You do understand I'm not your boss, right?"

Laughing, I patted him lightly on the shoulder. "Of course you're not my boss. I had a boss. Delightful woman. Told me when to go to the bathroom and everything. Point is, I'm finding myself at a loss when it comes to the whole package."

"As in?"

"You know, a benefits package. Time clock, vacation

days, insurance. The whole enchilada."

He thought about it for a moment. "I'm pretty sure the kids took the vacation days, and I just called you the other day about information I needed to sign up for insurance at work."

I nodded. "I know. I wanted to take a sick day that day, but you just had to go to work. When am I allowed to be sick? How many days do I get? If I take too much DayQuil, am I still permitted to care for the children?"

Husband inched away. "DayQuil's non-drowsy."

"I said if I take too much."

"Right." He sighed. "I'm not sure if there are any set guidelines for what you're doing."

In a defiant gesture, I flicked piece of dried chowder from my hair and cocked an eyebrow. "Oh, there are guidelines, and I'll find them. Somewhere there's an orientation package with my name on it, and I'll brush up on it in no time. Oh, and by the way, I was thinking about taking a vacation day tomorrow."

"You have to watch the kids tomorrow."

"I quit."

"If I give you a beer, will you stay?"

"Two beers."

"Deal. Oh, and bring the Cheetos too."

I threw up my hands. "I thought you just said you aren't my boss."

The problem was, I was still in workplace mode. Part of me needed to clock in and clock out, and the validation from a superior and competition with peers was still something I craved. Not overwhelmingly, but a pat on the back accompanied by a "Thanks for not messing that up" would be appreciated. I've never been a star-on-the-chart type of gal, but I truly think one of the hardest parts of housewifery is having every diaper changed, fight broken up, and desperate attempt to shove all of one's children in the car be completely overlooked by the outside world. This is a large part of being a mother, but when the cloaking device on the house engages around the person staying home all day, danger rears its head in the form of Invisible Woman Syndrome.

> **Invisible Woman Syndrome**
> *noun*
>
> The condition of believing oneself to be invisible, caused mostly by the subject's keeping the children alive, 168 hours a week, with no witnesses. Individuals with Invisible Woman Syndrome struggle with believing they've actually achieved anything within a day, and also have a habit of wandering outside naked, in the mistaken assumption they are, in fact, invisible. Subjects have been observed eating more Doritos than a normal person, for reasons still undetermined.

While I ate Cool Ranch Doritos and searched the internet for 'housewife workplace guidelines,' snippets of my past wove through a psyche currently submerged in meals dumped on the floor and people who communicated by slapping me in the face on a good day. Semi-fondly, I looked back on fake diplomas for passing a one-hour course on hand washing, coupons for a free candy bar of my choice on my birthday, and getting put in charge of five more projects because I'd shown I could barely put together a power point presentation on wood shingled roofs and the chipmunks that live in them. Insurance hadn't provided a whole lot of perks, but at least they'd given me my free candy bar a month late.

Validation. The longer I searched for it, the surer I became I was on my own. On a particularly tough week, I stopped a gas station attendant, two grocery sackers, and a person dressed as Uncle Sam standing outside a car dealership, to tell them how I'd changed a diaper without getting poop on the walls. After nodding politely, one person called the police. No one gave me a candy bar.

"But it was a really bad diaper," I protested next to the 2011 Ford Explorers.

Uncle Sam patted me on the shoulder and lit a cigarette. "You lookin' for four-wheel drive?"

"No."

"Move along then. You're blocking my sandwich board."

I was running in burnout mode and needed to figure out when exactly my shifts were supposed to start and stop, and whether time off included one or two weeks of vacation. Perhaps the recognition of my efforts would never come, but a person needs to clock out once in a while. The only people I knew who signed up for twenty-four hour shifts were doctors and guys who manned oil rigs out in the middle of the Atlantic.

So far, shift work had been rough. The day started with 6:30 a.m. wake up times and ended with 6:30 a.m. wake up times. If the math there confused you, it's because I'm terrible at math, but also because I wasn't sleeping. I'm still not sleeping. Moms automatically forfeit their right to sleep the day they bring home a tightly swaddled, cooing burrito or two. And it's not the kind of sleep deprivation you experience in college while studying for finals, either. Parental sleep deprivation is more on the level with Navy Seals and career insomniacs. In addition to rest, what I didn't realize I'd also given up was knowing, if the opportunity presented itself, when to turn in for the night. Even as I type this, the second of two Chocolate Mocha cappuccinos from a certain, well-known fast food chain clown are all that prop up these sad eyeballs.

It seems simple enough. Keep kids alive, take care of home front, put kids in bed and enjoy life after dark. Originally, I thought the first year would be a little wonky, but a schedule of time off at night would emerge. But, if anything, I've found the evolution of reasons I can't clock out for the day have simply changed in size, shape, and limited-edition seasonal variety. The first year home, what I'd yet to grasp was that motherhood and housewifery turns life into a questionable Yankee Candle shop, where Insomnia and More Poop are the only jars on sale. Even with a coupon.

"But what about Fresh Linen?" you say.

Of course you want Fresh Linen. Everyone wants Fresh Linen. But that's never what you're throwing in your brown paper bag when quitting time comes around. That beautiful sunset at the end of the day always relaxes me into a false of hope. There's always a reason I'm on call. It changes as the kids grow, but it's never as simple as kissing them on their sweet little heads and gently reminding them that, unless someone flies off a bunk bed and their arm is hanging at a weird angle, you don't want to see them until tomorrow. The litany of reasons starts up pretty quickly:

Ok, I'm done for the day because I finished all my work. Nope. The newborn slept all day and is now awake and ready to party.

Whew, done for the day because twelve straight hours of listening to kids fight and dissect the mysteries of life is enough to test the patience of Job. Nope. Trash needs to go out, dishes need to be done, and this is the special week the toddler learned how to base jump out of his crib, stalk back to the couch, and demand a 10:00 p.m. showing of *The Wiggles*.

Rock on, I'm totally done for the day because my shins are about to give out and I was not aware shins could give out. Nope. The five-year-old won't sleep. He decides, instead, to wander the halls, crying at random intervals through the night. This is exhausting but also more terrifying than watching *Children of the Corn* in a leaky basement, while the solitary hanging light bulb slowly flickers out.

In the beginning, I was sure there had to be a way to get back to a time when I could email HR, tell them I was going home sick, and wander to the bar down the street instead. Staying home couldn't be some free-for-all where I just worked random hours and didn't have designated time off, could it? Surely there was some mistake. One night, after putting the twins back to bed for the fifth time, I decided to keep searching for an answer to my conundrum. The light from the laptop screen burned my corneas as I recalled a beautiful, sunny afternoon I'd spent slouched down in a chair outside the local brewery, reading *Twilight*, wondering how many beers it'd take to get to the story. All it had taken was half a vacation day and maybe telling the little white lie that I had chronic diarrhea. Those had been the days. Lo and behold, my search finally came to fruition. In a small link, tucked away in a minute corner of the internet, was a website dedicated entirely to the guidelines of housewifery. There was also a good chance it was an Etsy shop that sold hand-knit sweaters for ferrets, canned jams, and patchouli oil in bulk, but regardless, there was a .pdf I could download, for five bucks, so I gave up my fun money for the month and took a gamble. It looked something like this.

Official Housewifery Benefits Guide

1.) Vacation days

There are no vacation days. You will, however, be offered the chance to sketch, in crayon, any place you'd like to go. We also don't provide the crayons, but surveys tell us Crayola's "Golden Sand" fulfills a realistic rendering of any beach you won't see on a daily basis. (Excludes employees on east and west coasts, who see ocean by default.)

2.) Sick Days

All employees are required to work, even if they are dying. If a hospital stay is required, children are obligated to accompany the beneficiary to the nearest hospital and hit her repeatedly in the head with a bed pan.

3.) Shifts

All employees are required to work from sun up to sun down. Switching shifts with someone else is allowed, if the beneficiary can find someone who owes them a favor. Such as repaying the time the beneficiary threw herself in front of a bus to save the sub's life.

All employees are required to remain on call until they are too old or ill to report to work. In which case, please see #2. You are not allowed to quit. Quitters never win, and winners make sure the children haven't set the garage on fire by accident.

4.) Health Insurance

We're assuming you figured this out, but it doesn't matter because you'll never use it. But, if you do use it, numbers two and three of the list apply.

5.) Pay

Not Applicable. Have you tried clipping coupons?

6.) Jury Duty

This is the closest you will ever come to a vacation day. By law, you cannot let your children tag along. This means you'll have to beg someone to babysit so you can sit around for eight hours in an oak-paneled room, be asked if you're prejudiced against the elderly or dogs, and be paid ten dollars for the day.

7.) 401K and Retirement

Have you tried clipping coupons?

8.) Life Insurance

Try not to die. (We, as a company, recommend you not die.) If you do die, here are a list of approved items you may choose to have engraved on your tombstone:

"She should've slept when the baby slept."

"Here lies our mother. She died doing what she loved. Our dishes will never be as clean."

"This isn't what I meant when I said I wanted to get dressed to go out."

"You're blocking my light. I'm trying to read in here."

"I don't know. Go ask your father."

"Finally, some peace and quiet."

9.) Breaks

All breaks will be utilized to complete tasks employees

are unable to attend to while the children are awake. The choice will be left up to the employee, i.e., "Now that the kids are napping, I can either do the dishes and take out the trash, or fold the laundry and pay bills. I think I'll get crazy and clean the bathroom instead. The scent of Scrubbing Bubbles really gets my motor running."

10.) Lunch

All employees seeking lunch should refer to number nine of this list, while eating a sandwich or quickly eating Cheese-Its, until the hunger pains are gone.

11.) Funeral Leave

If it's yours, please see number seven. If it's someone else's, please see number three.

*Additional notarized copies of these guidelines can be provided upon request. Add two dollars for jam of your choice. Patchouli must be picked up in the shop.

There it was in black and white, the hard truth of it all. No clocking in. No clocking out. No pay or sick days. What on Earth had convinced me this was a good idea? Cheap wine? Bad gin? That questionable dalliance with working out? All signs pointed to Mother Nature and a certain desperate phone call about having to stay home. Me. I'd made the executive decision.

Quietly, I shut off the computer and wandered to the kitchen, where I met Husband. He pulled a beer out of the fridge, "You find what you were looking for?"

I grabbed a wine glass and clattered a pot on the stove top. "I did. Turns out, I'm not allowed to die, but I found a great place where we can stock up on strawberry preserves and incense."

"So you're saying you'll stay?"

"Well, I think we need to work out a couple of days where I get to replenish my sanity. And I can tough it out through most colds, but if I come down with Ebola, you have to take the day off."

He smiled. "Done."

I drained my wine glass and set it down on the stove. "Honey, it's hard, but I wouldn't miss it for the world."

Chapter 10

Cleanliness is Next To Insanity

"Are you going to put that away?" The sound of small feet running the opposite direction signaled that the sea of pots and pans surrounding me on all sides was now my own special treat. Which was fortunate because I am, and always will be, a sucker for cleaning up messes that aren't mine. For example, I can barely go into a fast food restaurant without begging to scrub the toilets or sit and figure out why the tampon machine is empty. And heaven help me if I don't slow down at a construction site, roll down the windows, and implore the foreman to let me help lay some flatwork, because the kids accidentally fell asleep and I need something to fill the only quiet moment I've had all day. As I bent over to pull pot lids off cabinet handles and yank a spatula out of the dog bowl, I couldn't help thinking dog food sticks to everything, but also that it was getting quite impossible to keep the house clean.

Like the bills, keeping the house ship shape had notched itself onto the old stay-at-home resume. Unlike the bills, however, if I didn't put in a timely effort, the house threatened to cave in on itself. Collections people are pretty hardcore, but they, at the very least, don't throw oatmeal all over things. That I know of. I once got an overdue water bill that smelled like maple.

Growing up, I knew what cleaning was. At least, I was familiar with the fact my mom did it, yelled at us to do it, and we humored her by stuffing as many clothes as possible under the bed. In college, cleaning and I still didn't see eye to eye, but, luckily, I had a ton of space under my bed to shove jeans, sweatshirts and half-finished drinks. Unfortunately, this also led to the Great Rotten Milk Incident of 2004, and I still get questions from old roommates who can't believe I have children. That computer probably also still smells like aging brie, but it was a desktop and it's completely obsolete now.

Shortly after walking down the aisle, tidiness finally caught up with me, and a thing called Pride of Ownership tapped me on the shoulder and asked politely if I'd take out the trash and hang some picture frames. I had a new leaf to turn over. After the honeymoon, I got home and immediately took a nap. But after that, I got to work, straightening, dusting, and lighting scented candles. My house wasn't going to smell like cheese. It would smell like Pumpkin Dreams and responsibility. This turning of leaves continued when I found out I was pregnant with the twins a month later. By the time nesting kicked in, I'd turned over so much foliage, I'd constructed a small tree, potted it in an adorable planter, and stuck it in the middle of the dining room table, so guests could look at it while they ate the dinner I'd ordered in. But, as it often does, life happened while I was learning how to wipe down all my counters within twenty-four hours of the last meal. Just as I'd gotten the hang of dusting and leaving a copy of Southern Living I'd never read on the coffee table, the twins became toddlers, and I started signing our cards, "Merry Christmas to you and yours! From: The Danger Zone. We're all still alive for 2012."

If someone had told me there was no way to keep a house clean if I stayed home all day, I never would've believed it. In fact, I probably would've gone so far as to pick up my gin glass, wipe up the water ring underneath and quip, "Oh really? Like how I just cleaned that up because I was right there? Saw it happen? Ruined my last good napkin and have nothing to clean my hands off with now that I've eaten a whole basket of taquitos?" To my inexperienced self, I assumed people who stayed home all day should have the cleanest houses. After all, they were there, reporting from home base, seeing the action on the ground as it happened.

"Ladies and gentlemen, I'm coming to you live from my living room where dust has just settled on the bookcase. That's right, the bookcase full of Salinger and Vonnegut I keep for show. The bookcase appears to be unharmed but, what's this? I'm taking a Swiffer out as we speak and cleaning up this entire disastrous situation. Back to you, Tom. After the break, you mentioned hula hooping Chihuahuas?"

Time and time again, people have complimented me on my ability not to panic. Instead, I fill that void with being completely overwhelmed, rending my garments, and crying in secret. As puddles of things grew, laundry mounted, and ketchup kept falling out of the refrigerator on top of me, I felt my only course of action was taking my concerns to the board.

"Board?"

Husband looked up. "What did you just call me?"

"Well, you can't have CEO because I took that title, along with the last Nutri-Grain bar this morning."

"Hmm, so those crumbs were all you."

"We have a problem."

"Yeah, we're out of breakfast bars."

I shook my head. "I can't keep it clean."

"Your language? Because I, for one, am tired of the dirty jokes."

"Nope, the house. Not to mention, you're ten times worse than I am."

"What's wrong with it?"

"People keep living in it."

"Right." He was quiet for a moment while he thought. "Wait, I'm a little confused. Are you sure we're not talking about dirty jokes?"

I began the first in a long line of laments about the territory I'd ventured into and why he shouldn't expect clean forks anytime soon.

"And that's why wiping things is stupid," I finished.

"I see."

I'm not sure if he did see, or if he was commenting on the episode of Wheel of Fortune behind me, but that didn't change the fact I was currently looking at what I believed was and still believe to be an insurmountable obstacle. The cleaning, in and of itself, hadn't really changed—I could still jam a brush down a toilet with the best of them—it was more that the circumstances of sanitizing and swiping things with my sleeve had been altered. Admittedly, when the twins were infants, I hadn't run into any severe difficulty with keeping the house picked up. For the most part, the children were stationary, the only person making and cleaning up disasters being me. And even those were run of the mill: dishes I'd used, pants I'd worn when I wore pants, and peanut butter sandwiches I'd thrown against the wall when lack of sleep convinced me I was playing horseshoes with Queen Victoria somewhere around the dunes of Sin City, Nevada.

Despite episodes of brief hallucination, everything around the house had been ship shape. It even smelled pleasant, like false expectations with just a hint of delusions of grandeur. However, around the time the children turned one and started falling, headfirst, into baskets, I decided to call a staff meeting. There were murmurs and mumbling as high chairs were pulled up and booster seats occupied. For the sake of propriety, I got straight to the point. "I'm not naming any names, but some people I know who live here and can't drive are making me look bad."

"Ma?"

"Yes?"

"Cookie."

"I thought you were the treasurer. Are you in charge of food stuffs now? Doesn't matter, we'll all break for a cookie and reconvene in fifteen minutes."

Once everyone was seated again, I dunked a cookie into my glass and continued. "Problem is, you guys are starting to do things that make it look like I'm not better than everyone else. That's a problem."

"Ball."

"I'm not having a ball. I just told you. Now that you two are up and around, it's getting impossible to make it look like our house never gets dirty. Are you aware that nine out of ten attempts at self-righteousness are thwarted by piles of poop and books thrown askance? Yesterday, the living room looked like a blind man had beaten a printing press to death and tried putting it back together again."

"Ba."

"What's a printing press? Good Gutenberg's grave, let's go get another cookie. I can't even handle this right now."

The problem with keeping a house clean that has people living in it every hour of the day, is that there are people living in it. That paradox blew my mind every time I bent over to pick up *Good Night Moon* or pull three skeins of notebook paper out of the dog kennel. It's not that I wasn't trying, it was simply that the children took it upon themselves to make sure every time I went to sweep or sanitize anything, they'd be there to make it as difficult as humanly possible.

You'll be happy to know then, at the time of this

writing, I've finally figured out how to keep my house perfectly spotless while children are around.

Kidding! That last sentence was actually just an exercise in creative writing. Gotta keep the mental muscles flexed. My house is still a disaster until the witching hour of 7:00 p.m., and I'll tell you why.

Baby Broom Riders: I've read tons of home care articles, and most organizational experts agree, the simplest way to keep a tidy home is to sweep on a regular basis. Once a day. Nothing fancy. Try to get that line of dirt perpetually left behind, or rub it in with your foot. No one saw what you did.

I'm a huge proponent of regular sweeping. I'm an even bigger proponent of letting the dog clean it up. The thing is, when I do intend to sweep, I make sure to forget to do it over naptime and leave myself staring at a crumb wasteland when whoever is the littlest wakes up. Usually, in a motion of defiance, I point my finger to the sky and say, "No, today at least the kitchen gets swept. The rest of the downstairs will have to fend for itself and sink into an oblivion of crackers and half-eaten, ranch-flavored rice cakes. The baby will leave me alone and respect the fact I'm tending the homestead."

Carefully, I sneak to the garage and retrieve the broom. So far, the coast is clear. No sign he's heard what's about to happen. And, just as I lift the broom to make quick work of the kitchen, the sound of stumpy feet puts me into overdrive, and I start sweeping like a Canadian curler on amphetamines. I try to throw him off my scent.

"No one's sweeping in here."

"Mama."

"I'm not the mother you're looking for. Move along."

"Ooooh." Fat hands reach for the handle of the broom, and, for a moment, we're caught in a off-time tango of someone who wants to sweep, and someone who wants to sweep but doesn't even have the hand-eye coordination to flip a light switch on in the first three tries.

"Why must we always do this?" I ask.

But, like any other baby broom rider, he simply straddles the broom, gives a final yell of indignation, and, using pudgy feet, kicks the lowly dirt pile back into the four corners of the room.

Possibility of Electrocution: After sweeping, vacuuming is the quickest way to say, "Hey, we're fun and sanitary. Just look at all the neat rows sucked into the carpet." This is actually a topic extremely close to my heart. I don't take pride in many things besides my kids and my collection of movie ticket stubs, but I'm a woman who can take a disheveled mess of Berber and make it look like a well-cared for backgammon board. Except when those very same children are unplugging the vacuum and trying to replace the plug with their own fingers.

Yes, I'd love to boast perfectly kept carpet on a daily basis. Nothing would give me greater satisfaction than to vacuum in nothing but a robe, while I hold the first of my five cups of coffee before noon, but it's usually the same kid with a penchant for riding brooms who sneaks up behind me and unplugs, plugs, unplugs. What our house usually ends up with is filthy carpets and a broken record. "Stop it, you're going to electrocute yourself. Stop it, you're going to electrocute yourself. Stop it, you're going to electrocute yourself."

Mud Trackers: In a sub-category of electrocution lies mud tracking, or, as some ancient people have referred to it, "Well, that's great. Just great." On the glorious days I happen to avoid electrocuting the children, they do me a solid by going outside, rolling around in the dirt, and dragging it over the carpets. Occasionally, the dog feels like he hasn't given me anything in a while, and decides to join in, by tracking paw prints over the children's footprints, creating a sophisticated trail back to my bed, slipping under the covers, and escaping just before I catch him in the act and mail him to Peru.

A Cup's a Cup's A Cup:

Ding Dishwasher's done. Look at all the clean dishes you have for the day. Yay.

"What do you mean we've already used all the clean dishes from this morning? It's only 11:00 a.m."

"What?"

"You don't need a new cup every time you get a drink."

"Fine, you can have the Little Mermaid cup because it makes you happy. That was the last one. Ok, listen up everyone. We're all going to share the Little Mermaid cup for the rest of the day. Anyone who's got a problem with that can write it on a piece of paper, stick it in a bottle, and throw it out to sea because I care less than the person assigned to draw the waves in that movie."

"How'd we use all the plates?"

"And no more plates. Use your hands. Or a piece of paper from the scrap drawer.

Bowls either. If you haven't learned how to cup milk in your hands and sprinkle cereal in it, I'm not doing my job."

"Ok, I'm running the dishwasher again. Try to help me keep the baby from opening it. I just stopped him from electrocuting himself, and I'd like to keep this one of those red letter days where he doesn't melt his face off with scalding Cascade."

5:00 pm arrives "What do you mean we used all the forks? And all the dishes again? What is this, an Olive Garden?"

Mass Confusion: In the gig of housewifery, it's possible to play a certain game of cat and mouse, called "I'll try and clean while all the children are moving around and need various things." This usually occurs if the person in charge drank her pot of coffee too fast, or accidentally stumbled into a full night of sleep. For me, these days occur most around the time I accidentally hear something motivational on the radio.

"Turkey is half off at the Food For Less. And remember to use your frequent shopper card."

"Thanks, Food For Less. I'm buying turkey, and then I'm cleaning the house with all the kids awake. I'm not sure where the correlation is coming from, but I did drink my coffee too fast this morning and I'm hearing colors."

Recently, one of these days snuck up on me, and I careened towards a basket of laundry, without stopping to think about the inclinations of the three people watching *Berenstain Bears*. Just as I picked up a washcloth and began attacking the grape jelly stronghold emblazoned across the tea kettle, I felt a hand tug my shirt, "I have to go potty."

I tried to focus on a spot on the handle and act casual. "So, go potty."

"You need to turn on the light."

"But, it's daylight. God made the sun so you could potty with reckless abandon during the day and I could go on scraping the peanut butter off the toaster."

"I need the light."

Surrendering, I tromped up the stairs and illuminated the devastation of the bathroom. "Would you look at that mirror? Before I knew what was happening, there was a Clorox wipe in my hand and I was trying to figure out why the toothpaste in the sink looked like Don Knotts. But not for too long, because that's when the screaming started.

Bolting down the hall, I stopped at the twin's room. "The baby fell over," the twin who wasn't on the potty sang at me.

Quickly, I picked up the baby and began blotting his head with the wipe covered in toothpaste. I looked him up and down. "Doesn't look too bad. Hey, would you know Don Knotts, if you saw him?"

While the baby thought about it, the back door slammed, and I realized the bathroom occupant was done, and a quick look out the window confirmed she was now running around the yard, naked. Charging down the stairs, I had just enough time to remember the counters in the kitchen were still dirty, toothpaste was stuck in the sink, and the neighbors were gone so they couldn't call social services on the nude child swinging on the swing set and shouting, "Nobody loves me anymore."

Upon making it to the deck, I quickly ushered in the mutinous three-year-old and threw her some clothes. After which, I stopped short and decided the deck hadn't been swept in ages. Luckily, the outdoor broom was there for the five seconds I needed to whack acorns from between the weather-beaten boards. On my last swipe, I heard a scratching sound and turned around to three faces pressed to the sliding glass door, reminding me they needed to eat for the third time that day. Two out of the three were covered in toothpaste. I dropped the task at hand, dragged my feet back inside, and had just decided to wipe the breath marks off the sliding glass, when a car pulled in the garage.

"Ok, your dad's home. Everyone be cool. You, act like you weren't naked outside just now."

After a minute, Husband stepped into the kitchen. "Hey."

I gave him a relieved hug. "Hi there."

"Why are you scrubbing my head with that washcloth?"

I shrugged. "Honestly, I have no idea. I just know I got the urge to clean something today, so I guess it's going to be your face."

"I see."

"Look how it gleams now."

If the last four years have taught me anything, it's that I'm pretty good at sporting Keds without socks. But besides that, I know for a fact I'll never be able to keep a pristine living environment while people are living in it on a daily basis. You can argue me on this, but I have half peanut butter sandwich stuck to the back of the living room couch that'll tell you otherwise. It's ok though, until I figure out how to stay home with kids and teach them how to freeze in place all day, it'll probably be two steps up from squalor and three steps down from a hospital cafeteria. So, don't beat yourselves up if your house doesn't even look as good as Martha Stewart's third pantry. We're in the same boat. But, on the off chance you've figured out how to get children to freeze in place for twelve-hour timespans, don't be shy about emailing me.

Chapter 11

A Day of the Week, By Any Other Name, Is Still a Monday

Last year, I sent out Christmas cards. The good news is that I managed to get everyone to hold still and grimace at the camera. The baby even frowned, before he fell over. The bad news is I sent them out a little late. While I figured the warm weather was a tad unseasonable for Kansas in December, I chalked it up to luck and went about dropping handfuls of mass-printed greetings into blue post office boxes, trying very hard to ignore the impatient woman in sunglasses and a terrycloth bathing suit cover up honking behind me. While I shoved a fat pile of paper through the narrow drop box opening, I wondered how much mail gets dropped in the wrong slot and shuffled off to Rockland, Maine, all because someone in the line couldn't keep their shorts on and wait for the five seconds it takes to put a Christmas tree Forever stamp on a generic security envelope labeled in magic maker, "Seasons Greet Us!" and deposit it in the right spot. Then again, I suppose I could ask someone from Rockland, Maine.

Truthfully, it wasn't my fault. Spending large amounts of time at home had the nasty side effect of not only giving me variations of seasonal affective disorder, but also the minor and annoying side effect of not knowing what day or month it was. Tuesdays melded into Wednesdays. Fridays dissolved into Saturdays. And Thursdays skipped over everything and evolved straight into Mondays so fast, I really wasn't comfortable with the whole thing. That's the thing about being home every day with small children who aren't in school yet, no distinguishable markers hold out a helping hand to tell you whether you should take out the trash after breakfast or put the flag on the front of the house and start barbequing hot dogs in the back for Labor Day. And if you do get confused and light the grill before 8:00 a.m. on a generic work day, people talk or jump straight to calling social services.

My time had begun to exist in a void, an occurrence one would think could be quickly remedied by the cell phones, computers, and the ever-faithful wall calendar inhabiting the kitchen, but nay, the void kept sucking things into it, and time disappeared. To some extent, I considered this newfound phenomena to be somewhat freeing on the level of forgetting whether I'd been in the same t-shirt for two or four days, but on the spectrum of why the neighbors were raking their leaves when it was only May, I felt disturbed and concerned that I too needed to hire a May leaf raker. When I wandered out and questioned one of my sweet, elderly neighbors about a suggested course of action, she told me it was September and suggested that putting on a bra, before I went to buy a rake, was a step in the right direction.

"And you're sure it's fall?" I asked dubiously.

"Real sure, Mrs. Kellerman. And you missed the end-of-summer block social."

"I see. Were you handing out free rakes, perchance?"

"No, hot dogs. It was Labor Day."

"Right."

The only measurement of time I truly recognize anymore is the standard amount of hours in a day, one hundred sixty eight, punctuated by the sun rising and setting on my confused face. It stands to reason I'll get over this the longer I stay home, but, point of fact, it's been five years since the day I decided to be a homemaker, and I woke up thinking today was Wednesday. It's Tuesday. Luckily, I've come up with a system that divides the week into segments I can easily identify and use to guide me towards the right times to buy toilet paper and look for the cat, after he's been gone too long hunting...or knocking over banks. His private life is a mystery to me. This system is called The Seven Mondays.

At its core, The Seven Mondays takes my regular week and gives it more honesty. Broken down on this simple template, this is what my calendar looks like:

First Monday of the week, Second Monday, Third Monday, Fourth Monday, Fifth Monday, Sixth Monday and Seventh Monday. (Sunday is still the Sabbath, but, as I'm given a brief break for church and then thrown, headlong, back into my regular duties, it's included in the system.)

Actually, church is the one marker that lets me know another week of Mondays is about to kick off, so it's not only holy to me but essential to figuring out why Husband has gotten out of bed and randomly left me at 6:00 a.m. again. Before I figured out to use Sunday as a cue, I used to blindside Husband with accusations, accusing him of fun things he was clearly sneaking off to do before sunrise. One morning, I awoke particularly crazy-eyed and grabbed the back of his pajama pants as he attempted to exit the bed in the dark.

"Where do you think you're going?"

"To work."

"On a Sunday?"

"It's Tuesday."

I wound the plaid fabric around my fist. "If it's Tuesday, then why are you sneaking around in the dark? You're obviously off to go do something enthralling like get a latte by yourself and drive around the city aimlessly."

"You do that?"

I shook my bed head and a ratty dreadlock poked me in the eye. "Maybe. It's not important."

"You need a calendar or something. It's Tuesday. You're crazy. And I'm going to work."

He did his best to claw for the doorknob, and I unwound my hand slightly. "Are you taking the kids?"

"No, why?"

"No reason. I just like to check. Have a good…what was it?"

"Tuesday."

"Right. That. Au revoir."

I'm not saying Husband doesn't do the same thing, day in and day out, like I do, but his interaction with people on the outside and a boss who lets him know overtime's on Saturday tend to keep him on track with knowing what stage of the week he's currently occupying. People at work have birthdays and say things like, "Hey, my birthday's on Wednesday. Don't forget to surprise me with a cake." Or, "Remember the office camping trip you can't come with us on? That's on Friday." When I was still in insurance, my favorite catch phrase to clue me in to how many days I had left of looking like I was taking phone calls was, "Hey, hot shot. Got your performance review in. Don't be late on Friday, so you can find out if you still have a job or not. The powers that be saw you staring into space and eating Corn Nuts."

Unless I get wild hair and leave the house, housewifery provides me with very little opportunity to know exactly what sort of Ground Hog Day I've attracted this time. Going to the calendar takes time and usually results in me trying to figure out if the white square I was on yesterday is the same white square I'm on currently. This results in little chicken scratchings, marking my way through the forest of undistinguishable dates, and smears of peanut butter denoting where I was eating a sandwich and trying to figure out whether it was Presidents' Day. Because if it wasn't a national holiday, I'd finally scared the mailman away for good with Braless Second Monday. (As far as I know, he's still assigned here. Which is good, because I'll forget to make dinner at five, if I don't remember to stalk him at four.)

Considering the evidence and shoddy anecdotes above, dividing the week into all Mondays makes the most sense. No days to remember. No ancient Norse prefixes to get me down. Thor's Day? How about this day is the exact same as the day before it, and it doesn't need any fancy treatment or civilized nomenclature. As the Mad Hatter once said, "We're all Mondays here."

"But why a week of Mondays? Why not a week of Fridays or Hump Days?" you ask. (As an aside, a week of Hump Days was quickly taken off the table, due mainly to how ridiculously creepy it sounds. If I owned camels, it would've been considered more seriously.) The main reason for this is because weekends don't exist inside the void. Weekends, or the Holy Grail of being single, used to be cause for celebration. Two whole days marked the end of a week filled with angry customers who wanted to know why I didn't want to insure their wood shingle roof and three prior fire claims. Two days of complete sleep. Two days of watching TV and trying to remember my password to the local pizza place's website. Driving to get food? Nope, those seven seasons of *Gilmore Girls* weren't going to watch themselves.

The Seven Monday System sets the precedent for the rest of the week and doesn't get my hopes up unnecessarily. For example, where Friday used to exist, now sits a toddler who kisses me goodnight with promises of a quarter-night's sleep and slapping me awake for breakfast the next day, at six. No going out to bars, no hanging out in restaurants until closing time. Those activities require a full ten-hour recovery time the following day. In direct opposition, while not completely unbearable, the void promises no sleeping in and a solid chance, because my eyes haven't opened yet, that I'll be handing out frozen waffles to anyone who'll take one. Children are born without the urge to sleep in. They treat every day like a Monday, and, because they also feel every day should be a twelve-to-fifteen hour day, and you're their main source of food, transportation, and cartoons, you are now the proud owner of seven Mondays.

Initially, I began this chapter by stating that I'd come up with a week of Mondays, but by the last paragraph, you've probably discovered I was simply covering for my children because I love them, but also because they'll choose my nursing home. It doesn't change the fact that a typical Saturday night around the house is comprised not of brushing my hair and setting my GPS towards social interaction, but of playing multiple games of, "Which one of the children just screamed in their sleep? You go. No, I'll go because you went last time. Wait, I stay home all day, you go. Fine, I'll go, but don't eat all the Corn Nuts while I'm gone. Seriously, I counted that pile."

Husband and I recently took to playing chess, but whether we played during the week or I won both those games last Saturday is a mystery to me. He maintains I lost both, but I honestly have no idea. I think he cheated, regardless. The lack of a weekend has officially disoriented me, and I'm pretty sure he knocked my queen off the coffee table when one of the kids wandered out of their room, claiming a shark ate their pillow, distracting me from the board. That's the thing about housewifery: being home seven days a week not only erases one's sense of time, but also throws hyper-vigilance into such a state of overdrive, it does a sufficient job convincing grown women that Great Whites inhabit the bunk beds of the Midwest. Where relaxation used to reside, now sits a woman who mumbles, "But was it a Great White or a Hammer Head?"

For the most part, being sucked into this timeless void hasn't caused much damage. I'm almost certain I'm not missed at most baby showers or bachelorette parties or the get-togethers at the White House. Social engagements have mostly faded into the great beyond, which would bother me more if the rest of my friends hadn't fallen into voids of their own. Thankfully, most of them have kids and appreciate thoughtful gestures, like Christmas cards in July and May Day baskets in September. As luck would have it, I ran into an old acquaintance of mine the other day, and we were both over the moon at the chance to not only reconnect, but figure out what year it was.

I ran to hug her. "Well don't you look gorgeous? I don't think I've seen you since graduation."

"We talked last week," she said.

"Oh."

"How are the kids?"

I beamed. "Great. How is yours? Is he crawling yet?"

"Jimmy started Kindergarten last week. By the way, you look great for having that baby a month ago."

I shrugged. "I actually had him two years ago, but wearing maternity pants in public is still kind of my thing.

"I see. Well, we should get together soon. Let the kids play and all that. By the way, John was just telling me how much he liked your Christmas card. It was a little early, though."

"Yeah, I kind of got my months mixed up, but I'm thinking about throwing a holiday party anyway. What do you say? Throw some hamburgers on the grill while we decorate the tree?"

"Sounds good to me. I'll bring the teether I bought for your new little guy."

I nodded. "He did run up and bite me on the thigh the other day, so I guess that would be good. Hurt like hell. Anywho, grab your tinsel and come on over."

"Next week?"

"Next week."

We never succeeded in meeting up, but I'm going to do my best to send her a birthday card only two months late this year.

My single friends and friends without kids have more or less accepted the fact I can no longer distinguish the date or my position in the week, and have taken it upon themselves to send thoughtful notes my way:

Hey Paige!

We missed you at this year's Christmas party, but thank you for the beautiful Easter card we received the next day.

Love,
The Smiths

Dear Kellermans,

You're invited to a surprise party for Dan on Saturday! (Paige, this is the sixth Monday of the week. We can send someone to pick you up, so you don't walk in on Sunday morning yelling, "Shots for everyone!" like you did the day after Stephanie's baby shower.

Love,
Amanda
P.S. I heard her family promised not to press charges. Great news.

Dear Paige,

Loving the house warming gift you sent Jack and me. We've actually been here for six years next month, but Fresh Linen candles are always a nice surprise on a regular, old Tuesday.

All the best,
Jessica

All things considered, the same routine every day of the week hasn't done serious damage. There are worse things in life than a toddler drill sergeant kicking me out of bed every Monday of the week. For instance, some sloths only have three toes, and that seems like an especially difficult way to trudge through one's existence. How much can you really do with three toes? (Ok, I just checked Wikipedia, and it seems they're actually pretty self-reliant animals.) Regardless, not ever knowing the precise day of the week is a small price to pay for not having to wear a bra on a regular basis. That, and I can get you your Christmas cards six months early, so don't be afraid to drop me your address. Then again, let me check, I might already have it written down and stuffed under an unused calendar somewhere.

Chapter 12

And Then We Just Stared At Each Other

At its core, housewifery is really the business of raising humans. This is terrifying for two reasons. One, because the job requires an individual to spend massive amounts of time around humans who don't understand any kind of pop culture reference. And two, It becomes your sole responsibility to make sure they don't become the type of people who steal from public fountains or sucker punch orphans. People often ask me how I spend so much time with my own kids. I've given that question a fair amount of thought, so I usually respond with, "Why? Did they follow me? Please tell me they didn't follow me here."

Asking how I spend so much time with the kids is actually a pretty fair question. For instance, some days they play quietly and leave me to productively waste time on the internet, laughing at sloth memes and looking up recipes I'll never make. Other days, high-pitched sentiments like, "I think we should punch her in the face," waft in from the living room. Several afternoons ago, I'd just finished making myself a second lunch when, "I think you should fight her," stopped me from heating up twenty-plus Little Smokies in barbeque sauce. Silently, I crawled inside a cabinet and waited for small feet to run past the door. I still have no idea what would've happened if I'd given away my position too soon. I do know cue to hide when I hear one, however.

Occasionally, I'm obligated to explain the volatility of the children to Husband, the father who loves them but who also has no idea how they can spend an hour crying hysterically that they'd love to trade me in for a new mom, based solely on the fact I didn't give in to their requests for pie at breakfast, two days in a row. Granted, I probably shouldn't have tried to get rid of all the day-after-Thanksgiving pumpkin desert by dishing out healthy mounds at 7:00 a.m. on a Friday anyway (that's the fifth Monday, for those of you who are keeping track at home), but life's full of hard lessons.

"They hate me."

"They don't hate you."

"They said a mom who really loved them would've given up more pie the first time they asked."

Husband sighed. "Yesterday may have been bad precedent. But if you were eating it for breakfast, I guess it's harder to sell them on the oatmeal."

Relinquishing my will to live, I leaned my forehead harder into the phone. "No, they made signs and, if they knew how to write, I'm pretty sure they'd say 'We hate you.'"

"Signs?"

"Yeah, I can't really tell what's under the lettering, but

I think they drew a spear. They even said they wanted a new mom to show up tomorrow. Hope she doesn't mind having her coffee stirred by little fists. Maybe I should leave a note."

"You're doing a great job," he reassured me. Stay strong and don't let them walk all over you."

"They already did."

"What did they do?"

"Walk all over me. I temporarily gave up after breakfast and prostrated myself on the floor. They each took a turn walking by and stepping on my head. I'll never get the dent above my eyebrow out."

"See you at dinner."

I periodically call Husband for these little pep talks, knowing full well I'll never hear what I want to hear: "I'll rush right home so you can hop a jet to Paris." But it's always good to touch base with someone who has access to your social security number, when you habitually spend hours upon hours with three small children who might accidentally trip you on the way down the stairs. Not a glamorous way to meet your maker, but a possibility.

It's a tough task explaining that, while I love our children more than anything on Earth, a typical day around the old homestead can range anywhere from a shoddily reenacted version of *The Lost Boys* to a guest spot on *Whose Line Is It Anyway*, the range of emotion experienced going to such extremes that I'm left wondering why soap operas aren't comprised mostly of children chasing each other with pirate swords and shouting at the offender about stealing half sandwiches they weren't planning on eating. Now that's drama. Sorry, John and Marlena.

Last year, one of my dear friends experienced a lapse in judgment and decided to visit me while the children were awake. "And you're aware it's noon on a Tuesday?" I asked.

She laughed the relaxed laugh of someone pregnant with their first child. "Um, yeah. I can't make it out there tonight. Driving in the dark freaks me out."

"That's a shame. Well, if you're insistent, I'll get started checking for trip wires and seemingly accidental puddles of water."

"You're hilarious."

I nodded and clutched my phone tighter. "They say people in situations of extreme duress use humor as a coping mechanism. See you in an hour."

Overwhelmed with the impossible task of de-boobytrapping the entire premises, I threw my hands in the air and decided to crack open a new box of cookies and wait for the doorbell to ring. Five cookies in, I remembered the bell was broken and went to retrieve my dear friend from the doorstep.

"You have no door handle."

"I know. Come on in."

"How do people get in without a door handle?"

"They usually take that as a sign to go back the way they came. Let me squeeze you for a second and then we'll go make sure nothing's on fire."

Staying home has become an exercise in learning how children communicate, and also how to lie so seamlessly that they never suspect it was you who drank the last three Capri Suns and finished off the cookies, all while they were engaged in a fight to the death over who loves you more. It's a 24/7 linguistic study of the potty training set, and I still have no idea what my children are trying to say most of the time. Case in point, I'm writing this while one of the twins is sitting on my knees, talking rapidly, waving wildly, and clad only in Spider Man underwear I'm only about five percent convinced are clean. Experience tells me he either wants to talk about the current political climate or that he'd like fruit snacks. Some days around here are a grey area.

Apart from the lack of adult interaction, miscommunication with small children is the hardest part about staying home. Toddlers take it as a personal offense when they attempt to follow you into the bathroom and get turned away. To them, it's the height of manners to ask about your day just as you've sat down on the toilet. I've grown accustomed to settling in on the smooth, porcelain American Standard only to hear, "Where'd she go? We'll be quiet and find her. I bet she's poopin'." The worst part of the whole situation being, of course, that there's nowhere to run, no other grown up to deflect the impending hoard, and, in my case, no lock on the bathroom door. (I'm still nursing a grudge against the 1906-era builders who threw a lock so flimsy on that door, it probably broke the minute the architect's wife sighed on it because she was so smitten with the swan etched on the shower door.) Isolated and terrified, I usually try to deflect as best I can.

"Do you hear her? She's potty'n."

"There's no mom in here. Go away," I shout.

Tiny fingers wedge the door open. "We hear you."

Carefully, I slide slightly off my throne and try to nudge the door with my foot. "I don't think you heard anything. Cat could've knocked over the trashcan again."

"We know it's you, Mommy. We'll just come in and sit."

"How do you know it's me?" I counter. "We haven't even known each other that long. Is three years really enough time to recognize someone's voice through a hollow core door?"

Invariably, anyone who can climb stairs barges in and starts asking me the intimate details of what's going on, how I feel about it, and whether chips are on the menu for lunch. Oh, and we brought the chips with us, so would it be all right to eat them right here in the bathroom?

Communication is also lost when it comes to any time designated to wake one's self up in the morning. Nothing makes me miss my coffee and cigarette on the highway to work more than opening my eyes to someone sitting on my stomach, angrily accusing me of eating all the fruit bars, and maybe never feeding them at all.

"Before we do the breakfast charade, can mommy just splash some water on her face and tie her hair back with that iPod cord over there?"

"Breakfast."

"Ok, let me find pants."

"My stomach hurts so bad."

"But I fed you yesterday."

"Breakfast. Breakfast. Breakfast."

"I hate to inform you on what I believe might be a Thursday but could be a Tuesday that I may have to sell you to the circus."

After wrapping a certain someone in her princess blanket and carrying her down the stairs as requested, communication breaks down entirely.

"It's true, after she drank some beer, mommy ate all the fruit bars. But, can I interest you in a yogurt? Cereal? Toast I'm ninety-seven-percent sure hasn't expired yet?"

"I don't want that."

"None of it?"

"I don't think I'm hungry. Can we watch cartoons?"

"I thought you were so hungry you were dying."

"I'm fine. Can I color?"

Defeated, I go to pop the questionable bread in the toaster. "It's ok. Sleep is for the weak and people who don't like veering off the road at importune moments."

It's not that small children want to cause trouble so much as they feel the need to do things that appear to make no sense. I'm on day nine hundred and twenty-five of trying to figure out most of these mannerisms and customs, but, due to the frequency I run across them, a few of them have started to put off cues I've been able to decipher.

Cabinet climbing: Kids do this to feel independent, and to rip off your cabinet doors. Most of the time, people think I'm joking about how many times I've almost been knocked out by a child throwing open a cabinet door right in front of my face. But, I think we can all agree, three hundred times is nothing to joke about. On the bright side, it's comforting to think the kids have access to peanut butter and jelly, in the event I'm the only one home and suddenly keel over and die.

Not flushing the toilet: To small children, the noise a toilet makes when it flushes sounds like Godzilla coming to rip someone's head off. Therefore, they run instead of flushing. They also do this so you can question whether it was you who forgot to flush, thereby driving you insane.

Running around naked or just in underwear: Initially, this custom appears uncivilized and crude. For clarity's sake, I once interviewed one of the natives as she flew down the hallway in Little Mermaid skivvies and a smile. "Ma'am? Ma'am, could I have a moment of your time? Why is it you've thrown off the constraints of society and spend one-hundred percent of your time running free and wild?"

"I like to be comfortable," she answered.

"Don't we all? But, do you feel your behavior may encourage society to only wear underwear and throw off the bonds of pleated khakis and comfortable-yet-functional knit polos?"

"The baby's eating a crayon, Mommy."

"You heard it here first, folks."

"It's green."

"I said I'd handle it. Oh, wait. He ate it."

Eating Weird Things: Kids eat weird stuff. From the time they wake up, they're either sampling markers or licking painter's tape. Rocks, poker chips, expired international visas, it doesn't matter. I once saw one of the children eat a three-month-old ginger snap and smile at me the whole time. I was so struck with the brashness of it all, I didn't even try to stop him. Truly, I haven't given this topic much thought because I'm too busy trying to wrestle Twizzlers left by the prior owners of the house out of the baby's determined death grip.

Staring (or being Children of the Corn): When my kids have nothing better to do, they stand there and stare at me. I could be crafting my own thread out of finely shredded plastic bags, and they'd declare it the most fascinating thing in the history of man. Sometimes, they do this from behind the sliding glass door, or, if the weather's particularly nice and conditions allow, they climb up the side of the deck and deadpan me through the kitchen window. Most of the time, I keep scrubbing the soup pot and pretend no one's there. Other times, I tap on the window and remind them not to fall on top of the air conditioner.

Falling on Top of or Off of Things: Finely-tuned calculations have presented this cold, hard statistic: I say, "Get down. You're going to fall off of that and kill yourself," for about seventy-percent of my waking hours. The other thirty-percent is reserved for scraping people up off the floor, after they have fallen. The baby gets a free pass for learning to go up and down the stairs—kid rolls like a sack of potatoes—but, just today, I stopped one of the twins from putting his foot through a window while standing on his head, and then intervened before his sister could catapult off the bed and break her arm for the second time in a year. Although, in her defense, she did claim to be a "broken fairy" who was simply trying to fly. I have my doubts about the wire wings she was wearing.

So, it was into this environment, filled with plummeting children and cookies stuck to walls, that my friend stepped after she ignored my warnings and vacated the perfectly safe front porch. "Watch your step. One of the twins disappeared after lunch, and he could come flying out at any moment," I cautioned as she stepped into the entryway.

Carefully, she navigated around piles of blocks and halves of a pirate ship, finally reaching the couch, sitting down, and claiming an oasis for herself. Without warning, a toddler appeared out of nowhere and face planted in front of us. My friend's mouth fell open. "Is he ok?"

I patted him down and checked for signs of life. "He's fine. This is the one I misplaced, by the way. Now we're all present and accounted for."

While we caught up on current goings on and debated which husband understood the least about how much women don't get to sleep when they're pregnant, a symphony of cries and shattering things built around us until the baby broke my concentration by pooping and giving a look that said, "Well, woman. What are you going to do about it?"

"I should probably change him before the fumes kill us all."

"It's ok. I'll come with you." My friend bravely charged up the stairs after me, trailed by the twins and five hundred of their questions.

"Are you staying very long?"

"Who let you in the front door?"

"Do you want to see our room? We keep our underwear in the closet."

"When are you leaving?"

"Our dog's in the kennel. Do you want me to let him out? I'm gonna go let him out."

"Will you read me a story?"

"After you read us all our books, will you get me down some clean underwear? I think I peed a little bit."

Unfortunately, sacrifices must be made, and if you ever come visit me during the day, there's a good chance I'll leave you to chat with the small children while I change the baby. Them's the breaks. I can't wipe down an infant and remove toddlers from your ankles simultaneously. I'm simply not that good at my job yet. As I fastened the last tab on the baby's diaper, I sent well wishes into the hallway, where the corner of my eye told me that the twins had one of my only friends left in the world cornered next to the bathroom, probably making her wonder why she'd gotten the urge to introduce herself to me in college and let me anywhere near her car or her store of ramen noodles. I charged out of the baby's room in time to pull both of my oldest children out of the bathroom, where one of them was climbing on the toilet, and the other was saluting everyone with the blue plunger.

"Both of you, out." I snapped. The baby, wedged under my left arm, wiggled furiously as I picked up my daughter with the right. My school marm bun fell out as I whirled around to face my friend.

She began backing away slowly, heading towards the steps. "Is it always like this?"

I shrugged. "Nah. Usually, it's pretty crazy. Yesterday, I left the room for five seconds, and when I got back, the kitchen was on fire, the baby was sitting on top of the refrigerator, and I got phone call informing me I'd mailed an old family picture to the electric company."

"That's terrible."

I set down the baby and shrugged. "It's ok. That wasn't one of our favorite pictures. The good news is I think they don't really hate me."

My friend reached for her coat. "Hate you?"

"Yep, turns out, the kid who drew the spear was just asking for lunch, so it's sunshine and roses around here again."

She hugged me. "I gotta go."

The kids and I waved at her through the glass storm door and, when the car had turned a corner, I went back to the business of raising humans.

Chapter 13

Yours, Mine, Our Money

"I think I'm going to buy a new skirt." After I said it, I sat and quietly tapped my fingers on the table while I waited for a response.

Husband didn't look up from the baseball stats he was reading on the iPad. "Ok."

A few minutes passed before I tried again. "It might be kind of an expensive skirt, like the kind of thing women who shower every day wear. Has a lot of colors on it. Breathable. Very breathable. I'm a little worried about the sizing though. Says they only have small, kind of small, and "one size fits all." That makes me wary."

With a frustrated sigh, he looked up. "We've been through this. You can buy whatever you want. I don't care."

"You're sure?"

"I'm sure."

"You're sure you're sure? Because chevron is pretty trendy right now, and there's a good chance I won't be able to return this if it doesn't fit."

He rolled his eyes. "I told you, any money coming into

the house is both of ours. We have one account and one income. If you need something, you don't have to run it by me."

Ugh, the man understood nothing. Since the age of thirteen, I'd been supporting myself financially. Babysitter, grocery checker, roll bin filler at a bakery, they'd all been lucrative, if questionable when it came to how much free icing I was actually allowed to eat after I'd finished plopping the croissants into their plastic tubs. My parents had emphasized independence at a pretty early age, my mother never being one to shy away from dropping a stack of applications practically on top of me.

"But I'm only fourteen," I'd objected at the time.

She nodded. "It's never too early to learn how to buy your own underwear."

Really, it had all been small potatoes until I got the job as the youngest historical interpreter the county had ever had on its payroll. My mother always had faith. "Just keep doing the grunt work, and some day they'll let you dress up as a 1908 school marm too. This volunteer work with the Cold War exhibit should pay off soon."

Nothing like keeping your nose to the grindstone and your pointer finger waving patrons through the fake bomb shelter and onward toward the 1950-era, sea foam green Bellaire parked next to the bathrooms. But it did pay off, and pretty soon, I had my own wig and an official paycheck. I was seventeen years old and made sixteen dollars an hour. Life was good. I had to wear unbreathable wool a lot, but life was good.

College brought with it a series of jobs: work study in the library, a stint at a diner, bartending at a VFW and making Seven and Seven's for veterans, but it wasn't until I graduated that I sold out and started making real money. Insurance was horrible, but the paychecks had a shiny quality about them that whispered of decimal points moving ever farther to the right and absolutely no comprehension of why so much was taken out in taxes. Still, I was taking home at least some of those frog skins and spending them on whatever I wanted. I worked hard for the money and that meant my guilt-free purchases of People Magazine, cases of Red Bull, and ridiculously-priced stilettos were all mine. I hated my job, but I'd earned all those things.

But I'd promptly left my life of financial independence behind when I decided to stay home and become the primary adult responsible for not letting the children play in the street. Subsequently, when it came to buying things for myself, the feeling of guilt that crept up clung tighter than panty hose in a sauna. Had I really earned it? Maybe. How much money had I made that week? None. At least none I was aware of. There was a small chance Blockbuster had resurrected and those stocks had paid off. But I deserved it, didn't I? Twice that week, I'd caught a kid flying off the top of the refrigerator. That had to be worth something. I turned back to Husband. "Ok, I'm buying it."

"Buying what?"

"You may not realize this, but I didn't let the kids get

hit by a car even once this week, so I think we can all I agree I deserve this skirt."

"Sounds good."

"And I know what you're thinking, it's chevron and it'll date itself in the next two years, but the amount of lycra is really selling me on the whole thing."

"That sounds great, honey. Can't wait to see you in it."

I clacked out the credit card numbers by memory. "Your reservations are understandable, but just wait to see it before you make any judgments. And it's only thirty dollars."

"Just buy it."

"You're sure? It says I can't exchange it. According to this chart, a medium should fit like a small, and large fits true to size, if I'm a resident of Iceland. I'll just pick a medium/small and be done with it."

"You're driving me insane."

Now that I was splitting money someone else was earning fifty-fifty, trying to justify the things I bought became routine. Deep down, I knew I'd earned it. After all, I was putting in a full seven days wondering why the children were waking me up by putting their fingers in my nose, but the hang up came when dwelling on the paycheck. I'd always had someone else put a price tag on the work I was doing. For years, a person in a back office had carefully calculated how much saying "I'm sorry, but nothing in the bomb shelter is for sale" and declining ten insurance policies an hour was worth. I punched a clock, wrote on a time card, swiped an id badge, or someone else's id badge because I perpetually forgot mine under the car seat, next to the five empty cans of Red bull. Regardless, another human being dictated the worth of my time, and being the lazy person I am, I welcomed it and didn't ask for the details on the extra tax for "Unauthorized Smiling."

But what was the rate for housewives? Equating my daily tasks to fiscal compensation was tougher than I'd originally thought it would be. I'd been dropped into a paradoxical tree in the woods situation with fewer trees and more poop. If there wasn't anyone paying a housewife for her work, was it really work? A nervous tick I'd developed in my right eye told me the answer was yes. Like an idiot, I took my problems to the dog.

"The thing is, I'm pretty sure I'm doing work, but what kind exactly?" Gently, I set my beer on the coffee table and waited for some type of wisdom.

"I'm not sure why I'm asking someone who doesn't even know the meaning of work."

"Are you listening?"

Sounds of dog farts

"Whatever. The point is, I need to figure out what the speculative pay grade would be for this staying at home jazz. Then I'll know what portion of the income I can spend without feeling guilty."

More farts

"Ok, great meeting. Thanks."

Over the next few weeks, I set to work trying to nail down a profession fairly close to my now-chosen line of work.

Things Closest to What I Do From 6:30 a.m. to 7:00 p.m.

Accountant: Am expected not to overdraft bank account and pay bills mostly on time. Still don't know what 401K stands for, however. Possibly "Four hundred and one Kimono Dragons." Dragons are green like money, but jury's still out. Salary: $80,000. Could justify new and only bra for winter.

Nanny: Responsible for keeping children alive, fed, and happy (?) for duration of day, seven days a week. Pay varies depending on employer. I hear Brad and Angelina shell out $200,000 a year, but Rachel Ray pays mostly in lemon bars and sheet cake. Salary could justify new underwear for next year.

Housekeeper: Keep house clean. Not sure if I can factor this one in for a new sweater. The kids I'm nannying for just poured out an entire box of Captain Crunch on the coffee table and put a hole in the living room wall with a curtain rod that fell down three weeks ago. Note to self: Stop making lists and go watch the children.

Zoo Keeper: Yesterday, I was bitten five times between two different kids. Value to be determined by future research into zoological animal bite lawsuits.

Cook: Three times a day. I don't do this particularly well.

Hopefully, we're counting snacks. The tuna sandwiches I made the other day looked like they were being treated for depression. A typical celebrity chef makes anywhere from $300,000 to $1,000,000 a year. Me? Probably nothing, but no one here has starved yet, so I'll say maybe I make ten dollars an hour. Could justify new boat shoes for summer but not actual boat.

After I was done making notes, I sat back and looked at my list. One thing was clear, I was dealing with a disturbingly mixed bag of jobs. Also, there was a high probability I needed a rabies shot if I was being bitten that many times a day. How was a person supposed to figure out an imaginary salary if it spanned such ridiculous categories and also brought the threat of hydrophobia?

Husband wasn't making matters any easier. His birthday was right around the corner, and dragging behind it was an even more annoying conundrum than my fiscal woes.

"So, what would you like for your big day this year?"

Husband looked nonplussed. "You're getting me something for the first day of baseball season?"

"Umm, no. I'm not talking about spring training. I meant more along the lines of your birthday. You know, the big two-seven. Most rock stars don't make it past twenty-six, so I say it's worth celebrating."

He shook his head. "I'm not a rock star."

"In the right light, you look the teensiest bit like Sid Vicious."

"You don't have to get me anything. Really, I don't need it."

"But it's special. How's about we do dinner, a movie, and a Hershey bar all to yourself?"

"That sounds like what you usually want for your birthday."

I looked away and started stacking mismatched socks I'd dumped on the countertop, sorting by most faded to holiest. "Possibly."

He patted me on the shoulder. "Honey, now that we're on one income, it's kind of like buying myself a present. Besides, I never make a big deal about my birthday, and you know it. Don't worry about me."

As soon as he said it, he knew he'd, perchance, made a small misstep. Or maybe it wasn't a misstep so much as the brutal truth. I couldn't figure out which, I was too busy gaping like a cod fish undergoing electroshock. "Are you serious?"

He looked sheepish. "Yeah, you know I don't need anything."

"You know, sometimes all a lady needs is a little mincing of words at the end of the day."

It hadn't been meant as an insult, but it didn't lessen the weight of the cold, hard truth. Husband was right. If we were sharing one pile of money now, what was the point of trying to give gifts? Gone were the days of surprising each other with something thoughtful. I mean, we could, but the likelihood of marital miscommunication was almost guaranteed.

"I looked at the account online and it says you bought a couple's massage."

"You weren't supposed to see that."

"And you have no business doing business with Golden Palace Hand, Back, and Neck. Who's the guy?"

"What guy?"

"You bought two massages, so I'll ask you again, how long have you been seeing someone behind my back? It's like seven years, three kids that sort of have respect for us, and a mortgage mean nothing to you."

"It was supposed to be a surprise gift for your birthday."

"Oh."

It was a pretty likely scenario, considering the fact we'd already become privy to each other's previously hidden purchasing habits. For instance:

"You spent fifteen dollars on cough drops?"

"That included cough syrup, nose strips, VapoRub, and two Cokes if it turned out I was on my death bed and couldn't make it to the fridge."

"Are you sick or making meth?"

Or:

"Is there a reason you spent two hundred dollars last Wednesday?"

"Yeah, I got this close to forgetting to pay our taxes. But I squeaked it out. No prison time for the Kellermans. Yay!"

"I shouldn't have asked."

I spent the next few days after my talk with Husband

trying to come to grips with this new reality of mine. I was completely dependent, an infantile, sugar-daddy-needing woman who had nothing to offer in the arena of present-giving or financial stability. How had this happened? I'd diligently slept through Viking History 105 in college to earn my degree. And for what? To become a freeloader who knew a lot about Vikings? Consolation was hard to come by, every thought leading back to my financial contribution of zero. In my sorrow, I even bought Husband a Happy Birthday chocolate bar, but ate it myself, instead, to stem my grief.

Epiphanies are funny things. Not funny haha, but more like, "I really thought the meaning of life would come to me at any other time that when I was stranded on the toilet with no paper and not a soul in sight. Oh well, the train of cosmic revelation stops for no man and probably doesn't know what Quilted Northern is." When I finally found my monetary epiphany, it looked a lot like peanut butter sandwiches. Three plates stared back at me and spelled out, in off-brand *Not Crunchy P-Nuts!*, what I'd spent the last few weeks sulkily misunderstanding.

Trust.

Methodically, I cut the bread into halves and let a simple fact sink in. I wasn't going to let the children starve. Nay, I'd feed them once, twice, as many as three times a day so they'd have the energy to follow me to the bathroom or try to break out the back door. When Husband left every day, he knew this. He placed his trust in me that I'd feed, dress, and keep the three most important people in his life safe while he was away. In return, I trusted him enough to take care of all the financial needs, and the burden of that pressure on his mind was probably more than I could shake a butter knife at. I quickly shoved a giant scoop of peanut butter in my mouth and decided to change my way of thinking, then and there. Pity party, over. Peanut butter party, just starting.

When the other half of this new, equal, business-like empire we were running got home that night, a new age had dawned.

I smiled. "Good evening, sir."

"You ok?"

"Can't a girl squash her man against the cracking, laminate countertop and address him in an overly formal way anymore? It's just, I realized how lucky I am to be in cahoots with such a good-looking business partner."

"Hmm. Well, you're really good looking too, but this may border on sexual harassment then. But before I go talk to HR, anything else happen today?"

I plucked an empty shipping envelope off the counter behind him and shook it. "This came."

"What is it?" he said, wiping peanut butter gingerly off my shoulder.

"The skirt I was going to buy with your money, thought about purchasing with my own money, but then ordered with what I now realize is our money."

"Ok. But I think you overthought it. Where is it, then? Can I see you in it?"

I shook my head slowly. “No.”

“Why not?”

“It doesn’t fit.”

Chapter 14

The Time I Tried to Take A Sick Day

Man colds. If you are unaware, for the male of our species to recover from any illness, he needs the following:

- One month consecutive rest
- All care of children signed over to their mother until the age of eighteen
- A case of morphine if it's a sinus infection
- A private bathroom and reading material
- All windows boarded up to rebuke sunlight
- Call button in case he needs more water
- Loose leaf paper to draft last will and testament

And that's just for the common cold. If Husband ever gets anything like trichinosis, I'm packing up the kids and moving to the Bahamas.

Mothers don't get that luxury. There, I said it. No matter if she works in or out of the home, a mother is on her own, left to flounder. The achilles heel she banks on but never comes, death is the only way out, and guess who's still kickin' it on this great, mortal coil? I also consider myself a true survivor, all that is woman, and an extremely non-perishable canned good.

When I first considered staying home full time, my plan was simple. I wasn't ever going to get sick. Actually, that's a lie. I didn't yet have the foresight to think that particular caveat through. But I did know there had to be some sort of safety net if I fell ill. Colds, flues, malaria—surely someone would take over, until I returned, radiant and breathing clear, stepping back into the light of my new calling in life.

Wrong.

Unfathomably wrong

I was so wrong, I wish I had the presence of mind to build a time machine, put that enchilada in reverse, and time warp back to slap myself ridiculously hard. But I don't want to upset the space/time continuum, so that's that. Nothing made it more clear exactly how misguided I'd been than when I found myself, pale and sweating, shakily gripping the sink ledge in the bathroom a few months ago.

"I'm dying."

Silence.

"I really think I'm dying."

Silence.

"Yep, someone just throw me in the street so I can wait for the next semi. Get the whole thing over with."

Little hands clawed under the bathroom door while I stared back into the mirror. "Paige, old girl, what the hell did you get yourself into? Also, how long are you going to leave that toothpaste stuck to the faucet? It's starting to look like a stalactite. Never mind. You can come back to that when you're not in the icy grip of death."

After waking with chills and a sore throat fit to kill a hippo, I'd been left on the front lines to fend for myself. Silently, I'd stared at the ceiling and accepted my fate. Doom. Pure, unadulterated doom. Two weeks before, the kids had all had it. A week before, Husband had it. And because that's where mothers fall in the cosmic pecking order of illness, I was now rocking back and forth, wondering whether running out in the middle of the highway or wasting away slowly in the corner while holding the small, wicker bathroom trashcan was the more viable option.

More fingers under the door.

"We hear you."

"Are you coming out of there?"

"The baby pooped, and he can hear you too."

"I poured the milk myself."

A few simple mental calculations, and I quickly confirmed, at the rate I was wheezing, my chances of making it to the interstate were slim to none. Besides, the children were all fast runners. It would only take them five seconds, tops, to track me down like a giggly puma and put a blow dart in the back of my neck. Slowly, I took my foot off the door with no lock and peeked out at the madding crowd.

My five-year-old held out a plastic cup filled to the brim. "Look, here's the milk I poured. The rest is on the floor."

"That's why I tell you not to try and pour your own mi—You know what? Doesn't matter. I'll be lucky to make it to sundown before they send the coroner around for your mother."

While I threw a dishtowel on the situation and left it to work independently, I reminisced between hacking coughs. HR had been a pain in my ass, but they had always given me two weeks a year to do whatever I wanted. I fondly remembered taking the manila folder and looking at it with love and respect. It seemed like just yesterday I'd rifled through monotonously Xeroxed copies of standard forms and proclaimed, "So you're saying, out of 365 work days a year, I get fourteen to do whatever I want with?

"Flu?"

"Trips to Pike's Peak?"

"Irish flu? I get that a lot."

"Because I have extremely low expectations for this career, this sounds amazing. Where do I sign?"

The needs of the children broke me out of my sweaty reverie. The baby wandered into the kitchen and threw his sippy cup at me. "Milk."

"Hold on, I might be able to wring some out of this dish rag."

Where had I gone wrong in the planning? My throat flared like the fire of Hades as I looked down at the toddler getting ready to head butt me in the thigh. "Any chance you're up for watching yourself today?"

"Mom. Cup of milk."

"You look like a tiny, terrifying bull right now. With glorious curly hair."

"Milk."

"Please raise yourself today. Thank you and Godspeed."

But they didn't raise themselves. They did the opposite; they followed me to the couch and proceeded to sit all over my body, until the only part of me sticking out was my hand holding the remote. Quietly, I sent a prayer through the pile of children, up to Jesus.

"Dear Lord, I shall surely die here. Between the chills, congestion, and the two-year-old sitting on my windpipe, the tinkling of pearly gates shuttering open in welcome of my sad, sorry soul echoes loudly in the distance. Then again, who am I kidding? Please forgive my lying, laziness, and propensity for making fun of people who wear socks with sandals, and let me sneak into the heavenly plain. Never in a million years would I have thought You had my end pegged as death by suffocation while watching *The Wiggles*, but I thank you for my time here anyway. Also, I'm sorry for the time I grazed that person's bumper and drove off. Amen."

For whatever reason—work, school, seeing me on the caller id and wisely not picking up—the babysitting resources were tapped out. Why or why didn't I have a daycare on standby? That was stupid. I was stupid. I just had to be the hero. Who in their right mind decides to stay home with their kids every day without some sort of escape plan? Quickly, I went down the list I'd made myself before any of the kids were born:

- Make babies
- Stay home with babies
- Raise babies
- Double check to make sure, if you get Malaria, there's a back up parent to step in, hold the kids back, and let you curl in a fetal position around the toilet.

As I said before, Husband had already weathered this particular plague, and, like the parent who works out of the house he is, he had had me on standby to let him sleep. When Husband started sounding congested, I knew I was on deck, but I tried to stay hopeful.

"You ok?"

"Yeah, my sinuses are killing me."

"I heard once that the best medicine for backed up sinuses is to pretend absolutely nothing's wrong with you and bravely soldier on."

"Just really congested." He waved his head toward the stairs with all the enthusiasm of a man who'd just been told Lifetime Network successfully purchased ESPN and ESPN2. "I think I might go lie down for a while."

I didn't see him for two days.

In the interim, I made meals, did bedtime, and reluctantly took a bite of Ninja Turtle macaroni the baby offered me. A bite that, no doubt, sealed my fate in the sickness category. Things were rough. It was no Great Flu of 2012, where Husband had been out of action for five consecutive days and nights, the sheer duress of it all leaving me to wonder how the first settler's wives had braved the same thing.

"Well Jebadiah, the doctor says you surely won't make it to spring."

"Indeed, Annabelle. Looks like you'll be raising the children, curing the venison, defending the homestead, and weaving the wool into sustainable garments for the neighbors who will give you a penny each for them."

"My mother was right."

"What was that, Annabelle?"

"Nothing. I'm gonna go get a jump on harvesting that wool. You know those sheep? They hear you sneak up behind them in twenty-two pounds of petticoats and they run like the wind. Try not to die while I'm gone."

"You're a hard worker, Annabelle. Please know it breaks my heart, but you can marry again when I'm gone."

Annabelle nods and pulls a small piece of wool out of her hair. "Well, I thought I heard the young guy who owns the general store say he admires women who can run down a sheep in under a minute, so there may be options before the fall harvest. Who's canning eighty more jars of peaches by themselves? Not this girl."

In the small miracles category, I wasn't responsible for hunting down livestock, but after spending hours on end with the children and wondering if Husband needed me to send in a triage unit armed with Sudafed and the world's smallest violin, my immune system was just shot enough to cough out a weak "Goodbye" as he left for work on Monday. And when I say, "Goodbye," I really mean I was shaking uncontrollably, praying the Angel of Death would take me, and, in a feverish state, called Husband "Rick."

"My name's not Rick."

"Doesn't matter. Go now and leave me to die, Rick."

Husband staying home wasn't an option because a.) we needed money, and b.) I hadn't had the strength to crawl over and hold on to his ankles.

"I wish I could stay," he soothed. After which, he moved suspiciously quickly to his car. Too fast. In fact, now that I think about it, it had been the power walk of a man who knew not to look over his shoulder and catch a glimpse of Typhoid Annie chugging along behind him on her elbows.

As I lay watching the children take the house apart, it occurred to me I'd never felt so helpless. It also occurred to me they shouldn't be trying to dislodge the steak knives or stick the dog in the pooper with my good spatula. Woe was me.

"Woe is I," I cried.

"Woe are you," laughed the children.

There was much woe in the kingdom, the kind children cause when they can sense their mother is incapacitated. Like tiny alligators stalking a lame gazelle at a watering hole, they know once-hearty threats are now croaks of no merit, and if you reach to grab one of them off a counter, there's a good chance you'll face plant your swollen eyes, nose, and sinuses into the silverware drawer that's been left open for no other apparent reason than to make you wish for death for the eight-hundredth time that day.

There are only two other times you can feel more helpless while raising small children.

A.) You happen to lose one of them and have absolutely no idea where to start looking.

B.) You have no one to babysit for you, and subsequently end up taking all your offspring to the doctor's office. On a side note, I'd pay big money to see that reality show.

Announcer: All right, Mrs. Smith, the rules are simple. Just take this cup as big as a thimble, these three children under four, and your already-waning self confidence into that bathroom over there. Bring back a sample, and you've won the prize.

Mrs. Smith: Will people be able to hear what's going on in there?

Announcer: Everyone will be able to hear what's going on in there. Even the people in the waiting room.

Mrs. Smith: What if I spill some while I'm trying to keep the toddler from opening the door?

Announcer: Well, as anyone who watches the show knows, points will be deducted for any spills, and you're automatically disqualified if one of the kids breaks and or writes on any of the sterile jars.

Mrs. Smith: You mean that basket full of tediously stacked containers with the permanent marker lying next to it?

Announcer: That's the one.

Mrs. Smith: Sounds good. This UTI isn't going to treat itself. Let's do this!

By this point, you're probably wondering where I'm going with this story. Surely, a silver lining presented itself. In the midst of massive chaos, was I suddenly delivered from children whacking my aching body with cereal boxes they'd just evacuated all over the bathroom floor, by some rogue citizen looking to do good and save a life in the community?

No.

Absolutely not.

If you look closely, I still have "Honey Bunches of Oats" stamped into my temple.

However, I did learn a few key things about parenting without backup, while sick:

1. Your children will laugh when you croak out commands. Croak them out anyway. By law, you're required to keep parenting even if you sound like Phyllis Diller in a rock tumbler.

2. When you have a sore throat, "I think I'm dying" sounds just like "Let's get something frying." Run, don't walk, to the kitchen. The children have already thrown a wrapped stick of butter in the skillet and are hunting around for how to turn the right burner on.

3. Kids don't care if you're sick. When they inevitably jump on you while you're beached on

the couch, throw hands over your face and protect your most valuable asset. Which, in this case, is your mouth. It's ten times harder to enjoy a gin and tonic if your jaw's wired shut.

4. If you have to throw up, do it before the baby makes it out the back door. Puke and rally. Social Services is on their way.

5. If you have diarrhea, please see number four on the list.

6. If someone calls to help, don't be a hero. Accept it. (The likelihood of this happening is anywhere between .01 and .1 percent. In which case, see number four again.)

7. Train a kid to bring you ice cubes to chew on or make into a cold compress for your forehead. The child will eat the ice before it gets anywhere near where you can reach it, but training small humans gives one a purpose, and purpose is the only thing getting you from Monday to Friday.

8. You're going to want to mix NyQuil with wine and garnish it with Advil or Percocet. (If it's spring, I find a sprig of mint works just as well.) Wait until someone gets there to relieve you before dragging the cocktail shaker up to your room.

9. If you feel like you're actually going to die, put it out on social media. Make it funny though. People like funny, and you'll be remembered fondly.

10. Write down how many kids you have before your fever gets too bad. If you start hallucinating and seeing extra children, the chance you'll end up rocking back and forth in the corner, weeping, is diminished dramatically. It's always good to have a ballpark figure no matter what the situation. When Husband finally comes home at the end of the day, it is nice to say, "I think anywhere from three to nine of them are in the other room throwing butter at the dog.

So what's the moral of the story here? Unless we're talking about my uncanny ability to know when I'm going to need a Reese's and stockpile accordingly, I was ill-prepared for being sick while staying home. So, my friends, if you find yourself in the interesting position of embarking on a stay-at-home journey, heed my advice and try to have someone you can call if you're dying on any particular day. I have a few people on speed dial now. The fact that none of them usually return my calls is beside the point. The important thing is I have them and so should you. And if you don't have anyone, just pray that you never have to give a urine sample ever again. That's a game no one wants to play.

Chapter 15

A Quick Dinner

You will Need:

Beans, cheese, patience, sour cream, ground beef, upper-body strength, salsa, beer, tortillas, a strong internet connection, tomatoes, a voice that carries, lettuce and a cigarette or alcohol of your choice.

1.) Start by removing your frying pan from under the coffee table, place into it the ground beef you forgot to thaw, and set your children in front of their toys.

2.) With the five seconds you've purchased with a stuffed bear and an empty box, turn up the heat and begin hacking at that beef like Dana Scully working on a frozen alien.

3.) Halfway through your frosty autopsy, drop the spatula, run to the living room, and have this conversation:

"Fat baby, did you unplug the internet again?"

"Bah."

"That's the twenty-fifth time today. Can you stop it?"

"Ma?" Displays now-dead internet connection wire in chubby palm.

"No no no."

"No?"

"Right, no... Crap... just stop...ok?"

4.) Re-set internet connection, turn on *Sesame Street,* and run back to the meat that's turned into a hamburger patty (It's important to stay focused and remember you're making burritos, not cheeseburgers). Chop-up patty into little pieces.

5.) Stop what you're doing and repeat step 2.

6.) Upon returning to the kitchen, turn off heat under slightly over-cooked meat that now looks like that creepy over-tanned woman who reads US Magazine at the pool every day. Remove all other ingredients from the refrigerator.

7.) Chop lettuce and tomatoes.

8.) Repeat step 2.

9.) Run back to kitchen when you hear the clatter. That particular clatter means your son is climbing the stove in search of a pan of over-tanned meat to throw on the floor. Really run at this point. It adds flavor. Add taco seasoning.

10.) Extract baby from front of stove and set both babies in their high chairs. Be sure to buckle them in. One usually crawls out anyway, climbs over, and sits on top of the other, creating a tandem eating experience.

11.) Nuke the tortilla, pile on ingredients, and serve directly.

12.) Open beer, take a sip, and listen to the sounds of Big Bird convincing your kids to eat.

13.) After kids are in bed, sit on the porch, nurse beer, light cigarette and wonder who came up with burritos, anyway.

Chapter 16

A Letter To Store Owners, From A Vampire

To Whom It May Concern:

I'm writing today to apologize for startling you and causing a sort of extended nightmare or emotional trauma due to my lurking habits. You've probably seen me around. If you need a memory jog, I'm the lady who stares in your windows after dark.

Nope, not that one.

Wrong again. My legs aren't that silky.

Right, the other one. The lady with the split ends and coffee stains on her Hanson shirt.

Your concern isn't unwarranted. I, too, would be uncomfortable employing people all the while knowing characters like me are bound to shuffle in one hour before closing and proceed to stare into space.

"What is she here for?" your cashiers ask.

"Why is she talking to herself?"

"Who told her leggings are pants?"

These are all valid questions, and I'm sorry you have to field such uncomfortable topics with those in your employ. You see, kind sir or madam, I am a housewife.

And, as such, I find it increasingly hard to sneak away and interact alone with the outside world during what many would consider "daylight hours." I've also heard it referred to as "the old nine-to-five," "nighttime's cousin once removed," or, "look, there's the sun."

Now that I stay home, getting out to do things with my leisure time, like reflecting on all the ways I failed as a parent that particular day or wondering whether I should gamble on the cheaper laundry detergent because last time I lost so egregiously is something I have yet to master. It's actually this lack of mastery and your inability to stay open past nine in the evening that are throwing a monkey wrench into my free time. Is it possible we could all sit down together and decide selling coffee, scones, and overpriced cookies is really something that should be happening until midnight? Possibly one in the morning?

Instead, I wander in an hour before closing and set up at a tiny table. It isn't until I pull out the pup tent and a stack of paperbacks that your staff starts to worry.

"Will she ever leave?"

"Was that a cable bill?"

"Is she doodling on those checks instead of writing actual monetary amounts?"

"Maybe she didn't even pay us in real money."

"She didn't. She just left fruit snacks on the counter."

Why let your staff think I'm never leaving? Instead, extend your hours now, to meet the needs of the war-torn mother who's just seen her eight-hundredth bedtime. You know what goes great with abject desperation and the lost dream of a shower before noon?

That's right, a biscotti.

Coffee vendors, bribe your people to believe what they really want to do with their time is shove scones at me after dark. Lower their expectations now, so that, after they get out of college, life's mundane shock will already be dulled by my 8:00 p.m. swan song.

But I speak not only to the food vendors and dispatchers of Danish, for this brief yet strangely long correspondence concerns both the sellers of discount wares and the dealers of power tools. I'm looking at you, supercenters of the world. To illuminate, there's usually one night a week I'm not thinking about food. An anomaly, for sure, but on that night, this wanderer of the dusk would prefer you let her peruse lip balms and cheaply-woven socks until, at least, midnight.

Throw wide your electronic, glass doors, lest I find myself locked outside your giant, uninspired warehouse, breathing not so much seductively as disturbingly against them. Otherwise, your employees reluctantly spray them with Windex, hoping they won't be the one to have to call the cops and fill out the police report.

"Let me in," I whisper.

"Are you homeless?" they call back.

"No, but I have nowhere to go but home. And they don't have discounted paper plates."

Oh hear this, Captains of Industry and dealers of glassware with frogs and kitschy sayings on it, consider extending your hours or, on a happier spectrum, never closing at all. I ask you this: What's worse, selling goods for twenty-four hours straight, or finding me inexplicably locked in your bathroom come 9:00 a.m. open time? I once stayed too long at one of your establishments, got locked in, and had to huddle under a really adorable patio set for warmth.

Also, do you still have that patio set? I forgot to put it on layaway as I was crawling out of the sleeping bag I'd borrowed, which would've been way easier if it hadn't also been filled with Skittles and paperbacks.

I know it seems pointless. Why humor someone who spends her days sweeping floors, never finishing the laundry, and fighting the urge to start a drinking problem? Pity, my friends, pity. You would do my kind a great good, and in return, you have the potential to sell at least ten more units of cheap nail files and two-dollar pairs of underwear. The problem of pushing the last three clearance-priced tennis ball-shaped salt and pepper shakers would practically solve itself. Profit margins? Let's talk about hope margins.

Yes, you'll have to pay more teenagers and college kids who are home for the summer or living with their parents, but to us homebound folk, you'll gift inspiration and cheap sunglasses we can't try on when our kids are with us. Seriously, it's very hard to be me, and the baby just snapped my favorite pair of aviators. More hours means more time we can hold clearance bras up to ourselves when we think no one's watching and size up the prospect in front of one of those flimsy wall mirrors. I probably won't buy the matching cami and underwear because I'm too cheap, but your bra section would flourish. Who else would buy the neon green one for $2.99? I'd consider it an honor.

All I ask is that, like a fine fall cider, you mull it over. Think not what you can do for your bottom line, but what you can do for a shut-in like me. I am but a humble wanderer of the night, in search of ways to get away from my children for an hour.

Sincerely,
Paige Kellerman
P.S. I meant what I said about the patio set.

Chapter 17

All My Friends Live In the Computer

I wouldn't exactly call myself a social butterfly. Actually, I wouldn't call myself a butterfly at all, because I'm a person. But, I do like to spend time at home, and after I decided to stay at home full-time, my social life went from having a pulse to being dead. There wasn't any soft, transitional time, it was just dead. I used to love watching the show *Diagnosis Murder*. It starred Dick Van Dyke as a strangely believable doctor. If he were to walk out of the TV and assess my social life, he too would declare it "dead" and then ask Scott Baio for help with the police report. (Because in that particular world Scott Baio had also made it through medical school. 1993 didn't care.)

I've already covered how lonely I was. If anyone ever tries to tell you staying at home isn't a lonely gig, just walk the other way. It's not worth getting in a huge argument to prove to everyone that you are, indeed, a recluse. But, you know what? Everyone needs a friend.

Yes, even you, shaking your head.

You're a liar, but keep reading anyway.

I needed friends in the worst way. The friends I did

have were all working, and when they weren't, spent their free time with their families, like normal people. I spent my free time hiding from my family, so there was something of a disconnect. Quickly becoming clear was the fact the constant isolation was making me feel like an island that ate Nutella by herself in the afternoon, and also an island who had no one who could understand what she was going through. Oh, I tried to relate to anyone in the house who would listen.

"Hey, dog. I'm lonely. Also, I poured your lunch and you didn't even touch it."

Dog walks away

"Nice talking to you too."

Part of me missed the camaraderie my old job had provided. There's something about huddling together, engaging in a mutual bitch session at the lunch table, that brings with it solidarity and sometimes free cookies thrown your way.

"Hey, Bob. Heard they passed you over for that promotion again."

"Yup."

"What a grind."

"You want this cupcake?"

"Absolutely."

Being verbally trampled on the phone all day is about as awesome as it sounds, but there was nothing like being able to shout random things at your cubicle neighbor, plan for drinks after work, or wonder if the stuffed bear on your boss's desk was an inappropriate gift from a coworker or a desperate cry for help. Possibly both. Regardless, there was an undeniable human connection available. Sure, there were mother's groups, play dates, and bars I could take the kids to, but those all required going outside and being super social. I needed something visceral but not too visceral. Mingling, but not actually mingling in the physical sense. Talking but not with my actual voice. Lucky for me, the internet had been invented several years before, and it stepped right in to look upon my quandary and whisper, "Shoe sale."

Oh, and right after that, it whispered, "Blogging."

Blogging hadn't really occurred to me, but as soon as I did a few searches and found out anyone and their ferret could do it, I signed up for a free account and was off to the races. It wasn't long before I began running into the same people online. Writers, mom bloggers, fiction enthusiasts, photographers, moms who wrote fiction about ferrets. Sometimes it got weird. But on the whole, a brand new world had opened up to me, and it was full of people who stayed home and used naptimes to talk about interesting things. Gradually, I began making friends I never actually saw.

Me: Well, look at that. @livesinbasement just told me happy birthday.

Husband: Who?

Me: Umm.

Husband: And they live in their basement?

Me: You don't know my life.

Actually, life was pretty good. People had things in

common with me, and it was starting to feel like I hadn't been set adrift in the vast ocean of housewifery. There were whole blogs devoted to it, each one catching an angle of staying at home I hadn't considered, or taking pictures of it I didn't have nearly the capability to attempt. Shiny, new, social living without having to put on pants. Why a website hasn't picked that up as their tagline, I'll never know.

Ever so slowly, I began to build friendships with people I couldn't pull out of a lineup, if I had to, but it didn't matter. I had a support system of sorts, and even though we communicated as silently as mimes gesturing through bullet-proof glass, the world didn't feel as lonely. Slightly stigmatized, but not lonely. Loneliness is a key factor in choosing to stay home. And, even though it's a daunting task, finding friends is essential to keeping one's sanity mostly intact. Here, "intact" means at least seventy-five percent. Well, seventy-three, but I like to hand myself a daily extra two-percent for remembering I live in America and recalling most of the digits of my phone number. However, while I'm ridiculously happy with my online life, I generally don't turn my nose up if someone still wants to hang out in real life.

Not long ago, I went out to coffee with some old friends from college. On a whim, one of them had decided we should start getting together so we didn't forget how to socially interact. It also paid to have fellow human beings to sympathize when we told stories about how we heard children crying in the night who weren't actually crying in the night because, by this point in all our lives, we were totally paranoid. While I basked in the mental glow that was remembering to put on deodorant, no matter how much I'd gotten on my black coat, one of my old housemates lightly bounced her brand new baby boy and recounted the tale of her also brand new loneliness at home.

I stuffed a cupcake in my mouth. "And how are you dealing with that?"

She shook her head. "Ok, I guess. Except for the one lady I chased down the street."

"Wait, you just had a new baby. Why are you running at all? After I have a new baby, I spend most of my time practicing my telekinesis, trying to will things, like the remote, across the room to me."

My friend sighed. "I was hoping she'd be friends with me."

"So you decided to challenge her to an old-timey foot race?"

"No, I saw her running down the street and ran after her to ask if she wanted to be friends. Maybe hang out." She trailed off. "Or something."

I nodded. "Playdates present ample opportunity for rehashing the stalking rules of our state."

"Yeah."

"Did you at least tell her you were a runner too?"

"No."

"I probably would've led with that."

Looking sheepish, she took a sip of coffee.

I held my hand out. "Cupcake?"

I can't really blame my friend. Procuring companions when you stay at home is beyond difficult. It leads to awkwardness, embarrassment, and in some cases, hunting other people down in the middle of the street. The isolation of it all is the true enemy, but it doesn't have to be all the time. Granted, this section of the book should probably be written by someone who isn't a card-carrying hermit. I'm a homebody and an introvert, someone who'd rather sit on the couch and read an entire series of books while the house crumbles around her. And even after the house had come down in shambles, I'd still sit there and finish that book because I may be socially awkward, but I'm not a quitter either.

But I feel it's my civic duty to encourage those who stay home to find an oasis of friendship, online or otherwise. Like to cook? Go jump in that cooking class at the community college. Yes, it'll be full of twenty-somethings whose flan sets up better than yours, but so what? Gamer? Find the nearest *World of Warcraft* club and go mingle in that tavern full of trolls and elves. Perhaps that friend from college who you think has a fantastic social life is actually busy chasing people down the street. Call her. Maybe you'll shock yourself by rekindling a great friendship. Or maybe she won't remember who you are, but the point is, you tried.

Pro Tip: Only call friends whose boyfriend you didn't steal back in the day and people you don't owe money. Although, you could possibly use the money thing to break the ice. Maybe not. I guess it depends how much it was.

True, I have to make myself go out and do things with real people, but participating in an online community came pretty easy to me. It might be your speed too. However, if you're like me, you probably also want to brief your family on the fact you've moved most of your social life to a circle of individuals they've never met. Husband was pretty much convinced, when I said I'd made friends he couldn't see, there was a high probability I was just typing into a word document and pretending to laugh at nothing. Which I do a lot anyway, but this was different. He'd convinced himself so thoroughly that the Christmas I started receiving mail from perfect strangers took him aback.

"What are those?"

I had just trotted through the snow, grabbed the waiting stack of paper out of the mailbox, and jumped into the car. Snapping my seatbelt, I looked down at the pile of cards in my lap. "Cards."

Husband raised an eyebrow. "From who? There's a ton there, and we've already gotten one from most of the family."

I shrugged. "My friends from the internet."

"I see."

"Do you?"

He nodded and put the idling car in reverse. "That's cool. Where are they all from?"

I leafed through the stack. "Colorado, Kansas,

Vermont."

"Huh."

"You still didn't believe they were real people, did you? Don't worry. They're really nice. And they know where we live."

"Anything else I should know about?"

Waving him off, I went back to reading a carefully designed card with a giant tree on the front. "I mean, none of them are psychos, but just a heads up. Oh, look at how big their kids have gotten. Can you believe it?"

"I'm trying to."

"Can't wait to hang these on the fridge."

He suddenly stopped the car. "Hold on. They all know where we live?"

Truly, my friends online are my saviors. Some of them are reading this book right now. I see you, and I'm waiving awkwardly. Once I felt like I still connected with the adult world, on some level, it was ten times easier to get back into the groove of talking to people in real life, hence my current coffee dates.

I guess my point here is this: if you ever find yourself in the position of staying home, don't be afraid to find those friends that keep you firmly rooted in conversations that contain big words and veiled references to booze. You're not a Spartan. Admitting you need someone to drink coffee with and talk about the latest trend in jeans is ok. It's not selfish to have a life apart from kids and housework. It's good. It's healthy. Another voice weighing in on your impulse buy of flares when everyone is wearing skinny jeans is a-ok. Your toddler probably doesn't know what a flare is. And if they do, it's because they've confused it for a flair for the dramatic and are currently prostrate on the floor in front of the cookie jar, crying hysterically about the injustices about not having an entire package of iced animal cookies for breakfast.

This is also an open invite to anyone reading. Lonely? Kids take apart the kitchen again? Shoot me an email and complain. I'm usually eating cupcakes and trying to figure out how the kids got a milk jug shoved all the way into a heating vent.

This is why we need friends. And I also need a new jug of milk.

Chapter 18

If It Breaks, I Buy It

It was the summer of 2013. I wasn't sure of much, but I was mostly certain it'd been roughly twenty minutes that my hand had been submerged in a bathtub full of filthy water, gingerly rooting around for a hair ball the size of a Cadillac. "Come on. Show yourself, you swamp yeti. I birthed you from my scalp and now I shall extract you." There were great dramatic sighs and much smacking my head on the porcelain, but the more I tugged at the wispy strands waving like disgusting seaweed in our shower stew, I knew it was hopeless. Liquid Plumber hadn't done it. The pointy drain un-clogger that looked like a medieval device to whip peasants had been useless. It was time to make a call. And oh how I hated making the call.

"Hello? Yes, I think a small dog fell down my drain. I need your help. Well, no, not an actual dog, I—sorry, humor is a defense mechanism of mine. In all seriousness, I think I have a Kodiak bear down there."

"Ma'am?" the woman on the other end responded.

"Yes?"

"We'll have someone out between noon and five this

evening. There's only a charge after our plumber assesses the situation and you agree to the work. And you're sure you can't unclog it?"

"As sure as the time I dyed my hair black in the attempt to have everyone take me more seriously."

"Ma'am?"

"It faded out all grey and weird. And then, by second semester of senior year, I realized I'd forgotten to dye the entire underside of my hair."

A throat cleared. "It's probably best you don't go back into the bathroom again."

"Right. See you guys at some ambiguous time in the next five hours. Goodbye."

This wasn't the first time I'd had to make the decision about whether or not to call a repairman. In fact, my repertoire of distress signals to various electricians and carpenters was becoming expansive and dually impressive.

Fact: When you stay home, you're the person there when things break.

Additional Fact: It is now your job to get it fixed.

Bonus Fact: You're now the proud owner of a hernia caused by the heart-rending deliberation over whether you can fix it yourself or spend the money to call in a professional.

Sure, you could leave it for your spouse, but the bottom line is, you're the one running the show, living in the house with the broken thing, the one who's most inconvenienced the toilet won't flush, and there are three people behind you who need to poop RIGHT now. Not to mention, the person coming home from work rarely wants to stick their hand right down the drain the minute they cross the threshold of the abode. Instead, while nursing that hernia, you stop and fill out the mental questionnaire. This is generally how that form looks…

How To Fix It Questionnaire

1. Are you sure it's broken? If so, how broken?
   a. "It's sort of broken, but if we jiggle the handle thirty times, we can still get some mileage out of it."
   b. "Yeah, you kids are going to have to use this old Tupperware bowl for a few days.

2. Is this something you can fix on your own?
   a. Yes. I not only got my degree in English, but also, through various extracurricular activities, learned how to wire an electrical box when I wasn't studying.
   b. I don't even know what I'm looking at.

3. Will it be expensive?
   a. Doesn't matter, my grandpa invented the self-cleaning stove, and we're rich.
   b. I hope I can post date this check.

In the case of the bathtub, I was fairly certain we had a clog we couldn't fix, so the aforementioned questionnaire deposited me at the not-heart-warming conclusion that someone needed to be called. And now that I'd scheduled that dreaded appointment, I just had the final call to make, the one I hated worse that the first call. The call that breaks the bad news.

Oh, you thought there was only the one crappy call? Shhh. Stay with me while I speak in dulcet tones.

No, no. This situation is always a double serving of delight. In my experience, the second call isn't worse than the first because your Other Half isn't happy with you. It's the annoying reality you must now phone, text, or carrier pigeon the good news that you just invited someone into the house to charge you money, and then have the other person claim they could've fixed it and that possibly, just possibly, you reacted prematurely. Husband and I have done this dance so many times, our phone conversations have become a veritable lambada of second guessing the other person. The National Ballroom Association has a patent pending.

"Are you sure it's clogged? Like, really, really clogged?"

I huffed out an exasperated breath and went through it again. "My dear, I don't know what's down there, but I do know I've groped at it so many times it thinks we're dating."

The line was silent for a minute before he responded. "And they don't charge anything unless they find something wrong and we agree to have the work done?"

"As far as I understand it. There could be a hidden fee for dragging the plunger upstairs, but only time will tell."

He sighed. "It's not funny. This could be expensive.

Maybe I can just take a look at it when I get home."

Uh oh. Time to run interference. This is where the second call is trickiest, trying to get the other person to believe you're not a complete idiot. You've tried everything, Googled all information, made an informed decision. You're sure they can't fix it, but they're not sure they can't fix it. In their mind, there's still hope of a simple, cheap resolution. But you're the one on the front lines who knows the gravity of the situation. Not only that, waiting until your spouse gets home means living with whatever is catastrophically broken until the end of the day. And then what, if they still can't fix it? You're right back where you were. Not on Paige Kellerman's watch.

"No, it's really clogged. I can't unplug it. That may even be the plumber now. Or possibly a squirrel throwing itself against the front door. Gotta go."

Quickly, I threw my phone on the counter and ran upstairs in search of a bra. I only had a couple hours left to figure out where one of the three stretched-out and faded Hanes sports bras had been stuffed. You may be asking yourself, why bother making the call to the spouse at work, if you've already scheduled the repairman to come out for a visit? Am I woman who needs to run everything through her man in order to get approval before she even sneezes? No. I can sneeze with the best of them. This query can be summed up in a simple mathematical equation:

Not making your spouse aware + Simple service call

that turns into an expensive situation = Epically blindsiding the other person, therefore making dinner super awkward for the next week.

I only like my dinners kind of awkward, so I always make the call, thereby hurtling the first hurtle in the first of the series of hurtles that is calling a repair man to your home. The whole debacle you've just entered has only begun, and there's still so far to go. The next step is sizing up the complete stranger you've just called out, and making sure they enter your home without getting talked to death.

"Hi, thanks for getting out here so quick." I swung the door wider so the calm-looking man on the porch could enter the maelstrom that had become my morning. He didn't look like a total criminal, so that was a plus. And before you think I judge too harshly, remember, if you ever find yourself in a situation where you stay at home, it's a must to size up who pops onto your doorstep. It's the difference between keeping the serial killers out and being able to state whether the guy who walked off with your flat screen had a two-headed dragon tattoo or just one, big ugly chameleon on his left calf.

He smiled. "No problem, Mrs. Kellerman. I understand you have a clogged drain?"

Two children began flanking the poor man on both sides while I answered. "Sure do. Not sure if the lady at your office filled you in on everything, but I was totally joking about the bear. I think. At this point, whatever you pull out of that tub won't surprise me. If it's the social security card that went missing in March, I'll be ecstatic."

He gave a quick nod. "Well, I'll take a look. Probably just something stubborn down there. And who are these guys?"

Sheepishly, I reached over and pried one of the twins off the man's right leg. "These are the twins. They, umm, get super excited when people come over. They also ask a lot of questions. You know three year ol—" But the queries had already started.

"Who is this man?"

"Why is he wearing those pants? They're blue. Why is he wearing blue pants?"

"Why do you have blue plants? Is that a flashlight?"

"Can I see your flashlight?"

"That's not fair! You can't let him see the flashlight and not let me see it! Can I have it after him?"

"Why is he so tall, mamma?"

"Why are you so tall?"

"Mamma?"

But it was too late, I'd already thrown the plumber over my shoulder and whisked him to an area with less questions. The second hurtle in this situation is the fact that, when you stay at home with your kids, any time there's a service call, you have to babysit and try and do business at the same time. It's like trying to…well, I'm not really sure of a suitable metaphor because it's just the worst.

Children shouted over me while I motioned toward the cesspool of a tub. I couldn't be sure, but it seemed like, in the time between my call to the plumber and his arrival, things had started to grow over the cracked porcelain. Was that seaweed inching over the "hot" handle? The world would never know. I coughed and tried to breathe strictly through my mouth. "Sorry about the smell. Again, I have no idea why it won't drain. I've been trying to stick this pointy thing down there and nada."

The twins broke free of my legs and rushed forward. "What's down there?"

"Did mommy do it?"

"If we stand here really quiet, can we watch? What if I just stand on the toilet? Then I can see what's going on."

Insert sounds of me trying to pull two reasonably-sized children back from falling head first into our new swamp.

He was either extremely kind or too perplexed by what he was feeling underneath the murkiness, but the insanity I was trying desperately to control didn't seem to faze the plumber as he rooted around for the cause our current shower dilemma. "I'm not totally sure what's down here, but it's stuck really good," he grunted. "I'm gonna snake it, and that'll probably move whatever it is."

I nodded. "Sounds great. I'll be fencing the kids in downstairs. Don't mind the screaming. They do that when they're happy or sad, or to express pretty much any emotion at this point."

A solid half hour went by. From the bathroom, sounds of scraping and delving into depths unknown steadily ate away my hopes for a quick resolution. But, perhaps there was light at the end of the tunnel. Maybe, just maybe, the plumber was inches away from whatever was causing me to smack my checkbook against the stove repeatedly. Yes, that was it. Hold out, Paige. It's always darkest before the da—"

"I can't get this unclogged."

It was always darkest before the damn. Wasn't that how the saying went? Or was it damn%&(f***sh%$@&t?

"You can't get it unstuck? What does that mean?"

Coughing, he laid out a diagram of his plan in the air with his hands. "Well, I'm gonna have to take the whole unit apart and twist it off like this. And then, once I'm in, I can extract the lever like so." His hands moved faster. And if I can just reach the bottom of the thing, I might be able to see what's down there."

"Ok, so after all that, you might be able to see what the clog is? Might?" I began swatting at light spots in my vision that were quickly taking on the shape of dollar signs.

"You all right, ma'am?" he asked.

"Fantastic. One of the kids just jumped the fence, but I'm good. If there's nothing else you can do, I guess that's the way we go."

Things that give a homeowner pause when having repairs done:

"I'm not sure what the problem is."

"I'm going to try something else."

"This tool isn't doing it, but I might have one in the van."

"This went way different when we were going over this particular scenario in class last week."

"I'm gonna have to call someone else."

Or…

"I can't fix it."

After another hour of taking things apart and banging against everything else, he'd prepared me for the worst by bringing me to the laundry room, where less of the general public could hear my screams of frustration. "But why? Why can't you fix it?"

He sighed and motioned for me to look up. "That. There."

"That cobweb? Actually, we don't go back in that corner much. "Looks more like a spider condo."

Out of the three wrenches in his tool belt, he grabbed the medium-sized one and used it to knock on a large, corroded pipe directly above us. "This is your main trap. This is also where the clog is."

I clapped my hands. "Well, great. You have my full permission to open it up and go to town."

"I can't."

Ugh, I could feel another call looming on the horizon. "Sure you can. Fixing problems like this is half perspiration, forty-percent desperation, and a ten-percent chance I'll make you call my husband to give him the news."

"Ma'am, the reason I can't fix this is because the main trap to the house is rusted shut. It's fifty years old, and besides, they don't manufacture this particular part anymore. You'll have to have brand new pvc run all the way from your bathroom and have it connected to a new main trap."

Luckily, this guy was leveling with me without talking down to my womanly stature at the same time. A common state of affairs, amongst the crappy phone calls one who stays home has to make in these situations, there's almost always one or two incidents where the male repairman assumes you're the "little lady" of the house, and can, therefore, be told everything is sunshine and rainbows, that your pretty little head was overreacting, and if you could find it in your limited education to make the check out to Man Who Speaks Down To You, that would be great because the office doesn't have a joint account. Most people aren't like this. I've worked with many a repairman who shook hands squarely and realized I was fully capable of running the business juncture and was also too smart to believe that the hole in the roof wasn't an "extra skylight." Bless you, ninety-nine percent of repairmen. You other one percent need to stop trying to convince me an oil change costs five hundred dollars and half of my retirement fund. I'm not buying it, but I will take that two-pack of pine tree air fresheners, because they're adorable.

I squinted and asked the crucial question. "How much?"

He let out a low whistle. "Probably lookin' at twelve hundred."

"Yen?"

"Dollars.'

"Right, well, I'll let my husband know and we'll try to get something scheduled. You know, after his emotional trauma subsides."

I watched the white van with block lettering roll down the driveway and disappear down the street. *Twelve hundred? Maybe he really meant twelve hundred pennies. That sounds way more reasonable. Should I call? No, it would ruin his day. I should call. Or I could assault him with this horrible news when he gets home looking for solace from work. I'll call.*

This part is crucial in the head decision-maker process. Do you make the third call and horrify the person at work with the large bill you're getting ready to incur? What if that news affects their work for the rest of the day and, instead of simply using the copier to make copies, they hit it with a baseball bat? Then again, getting bad news out of the way is like a band aid: just rip it off, and your love will have time to process the news and come home in a terrible mood.

What was that?

Exactly right. Nobody wins here.

"So, here's the deal." (I love leading with this line. It implies hope where there is none.)

Husband was quiet for a moment before he answered. "Yes?"

In this particular circumstance, it's best to tiptoe around the bottom line. It softens the blow and also gives the receiver of the news time to put down any object they could throw across the room. "I tell ya, this guy says he's never seen anything like it. Well, I mean, he's seen something like it because he's a plumber, and also because that's how he knows how much to charge us. He tried. He really, really tried, but we're a tough case, I guess. Then again, things could be so much worse. I mean, the house could be swept up in a giant typhoon and then we'd really have water problems."

Husband was understandably stunned. "What? I thought it was a clog? How much is it?"

"Twelve hundred?"

"You don't sound sure."

"No, I'm sure. It's twelve hundred."

"Then why'd you phrase it like a question?"

"I don't know. Sometimes it's good to put things in question form, when you're verbally ruining another person's entire day?"

"Well, this is just great." He sighed and then mostly mumbled the rest to himself. "I guess if that's what gotta happen. I just…twelve hundred dollars. I can't believe this is happening."

I felt terrible. Part of the head decision-maker's job is to feel terrible. You didn't technically do anything, but you're the one who called the guy out who just asked you to write a check that's bigger than three month's worth of grocery bills. Feeling like the bad guy goes with the territory. If the shoe fits the duck, you're f*cked. Or some wise old saying like that.

"Fine. Go ahead and schedule the work, I guess. You

can see the damage better than I can."

Somewhere, deep down, a spark had begun to glow inside me. "Wait."

"Wait, what?"

"I think I might know a guy who can fix this."

"Why didn't you call that guy to begin with?"

"I forgot about the guy."

"How could you forget about the guy?"

"I don't know, but I'll call him now. He might be able to get us a better price."

"Geeze, just call him first next time."

"Do *you* know a guy?

"No."

It was best to get off the phone before things got testy. "I'm calling him now. I'll have an update when you get home."

I'm the queen of my castle. Sometimes I settle for crappy prices, and other times I remember a guy who knows a guy who knows a guy who lives by the river and fixes pipes. Sometimes you have to dig your heels in, kick the other repairman to the curb, and do things another way.

"Hi, Bill? This is Paige Kellerman. Uh huh. I don't know if you remember me but—right, I'm their daughter. No, not that daughter. The other one. Well, I've never really considered myself as raven-haired, but sure. Nope, still don't think you're thinking of the right person."

Two hours later, and I had a second opinion and the work done for half the price. It only cost me another round of phone calls and pretending that the friend-of-a-friend-of-my-parents knew who I was. For the record, I don't have raven hair. I have perfectly respectable fake blonde hair, but if that's how someone wants to put me in their phone, then ok. When Husband got home, the drains were draining and water was headed the direction it needed to go. I'd steered the ship and, kick butt homemaker/businesswoman that I am, dished out equal hot showers for everyone that night like a delightful, steamy shower fairy. Which, now that I type it out, sounds really gross.

Managing our home's business affairs has gotten a little easier over time. The kids still ambush repairmen every time they come over, but I've gotten better at running interference. In the time since I started this book, I believe I've conducted, roughly, three-hundred-thousand business transactions with plumbers, sheet rockers, foundation specialists, people who weren't so skilled at foundations, handymen, and electricians, all of them a learning experience. Do I take any joy in being the one who always has to be the first person to stick her hand in the drain and whip out the credit card? Not really, but I am getting better at being assertive and trusting my own instincts. For instance, November 2014 marked the last time I believed that, just because someone had the right tools for the job, it meant they weren't going to try and get me to believe that a shim and a sham are the same thing. I also want my two-hundred-and-fifty dollars back.

That's neither here nor there.

The only thing I haven't gotten better at is the call. I still hate making the call. And if any of you are brave enough to volunteer, please send inquires to my inbox on how you can start a great internship at the Kellerman residence, which pretty much only includes calling Husband and giving him bad news. In fact, you're already hired. Now that I know how, I'll show my gratitude by unplugging your hair-clogged drains for free.

Chapter 19

What Do You Do All Day?

"Occupation." While people read magazines and watched TV in chairs around me, I tapped my pen against the patient chart and debated quietly with myself over what to put in the blank space. It took a few seconds, but I soon completed the mental gymnastics required to fill in the missing piece of information, quickly scribbled, *Homemaker*, and padded back up to the front desk to give the clipboard back to the waiting nurse. She smiled, took the papers, and handed me back my insurance card. "So this is your fourth baby?"

I nodded. "Yep. My husband looked at me when I walked through the living room, sometime in February, and here we are. I was completely snowed in. Nowhere to go. It was either that or rent a dog sled and chance the run to the grocery store."

She glanced at the chart. "Mmm hmm. And, just to verify, your husband is the primary provider of insurance because you don't work, correct?"

I sighed inwardly before I answered. "No, I don't work. Also, are the stickers in this basket free? I grabbed some for the kids, but I kind of want one too."

Like every other time this conversation had presented itself in the last few years, I didn't have the energy to launch into the litany of reasons I really was working during the day. Besides, I knew what she meant. If I wasn't technically employed, I was adrift without an occupation, labeled value, or accompanying insurance plan with swanky high deductible attached. I did have a new *Frozen* sticker though.

The question about whether what I do during the day is an actual job perplexed me from the very start. After all, people who have jobs collect payment for the hours they put in. Then again, I'd had tons of jobs over the years, but I was almost one-hundred-percent certain keeping the kids alive and taking care of the household minutia, every day of the year, was more involved than the six months I'd spent making personal pan pizzas and eating free nachos in a local food court.

One article I read posited that being a stay-at-home mom was a hobby. This didn't ring true either. Potty training a toddler and trying to keep two preschoolers from drawing on the walls with marker is relaxing, but not nearly as much as knitting or massaging raw clay into a beautiful piece of pottery. Most of my early confusion sprang from innocent chit chat I engaged in with friends who were checking to see if I was still alive, or when meeting new acquaintances at things like the token Christmas party Husband and I attend every season. December of 2012 was one such occasion. Between evaluating the plastic beautician's head I'd received in the White Elephant gift exchange and eating my weight in crab dip, I was introduced to a husband of a friend.

"So, what do you do?" he asked.

Nervously, I wiped crab on the dummy head under my arm. "Oh, well. I stay at home. I mean, I'm a writer. That is to say, when I'm not writing, my full-time work is raising kids for no pay. Now that I think about it, I may just be a volunteer who's full of imitation seafood."

He smiled. "Man, it must be awesome not to have a job. Staying home all day, that's the dream."

"It's dreamy. For sure…um, sorry, I feel like I'm blocking the cheese cubes. I also need to go make sure I have an extra seat in the car for my new head. Nice to meet you."

The main mistake I made in that particular situation was deciding whether being a writer or being a stay at home mom would be taken more seriously. Turns out, unless you're Stephen King and running a daycare, most people still view you as unemployed. But the struggle to appear relevant and as an active, contributing member of society was something I didn't know how to tackle. Was I relevant? It wasn't until I met up with a friend of mine and gained a little more insight that I began to piece together the cosmic puzzle of my self-worth.

"I'm just glad you're still alive," she said.

I poured myself another cup of coffee and shuffled over to join her at the kitchen table. "Why's that?" I asked.

"Well, for one, no one's heard from you in a while.

And two, I'm relieved the Mom Wars haven't taken you yet."

"Mom Wars? Never heard of them. Why, are there women out there assaulting each other with nursing bras I should know about?"

She shook her head. "No, it's more like a competition. You know. Working moms against moms who stay home. It's the great search for who's more dedicated. I'm pretty relieved you haven't been drafted yet."

"I'd have to be drafted. Unless there's free food involved, you know I never volunteer for anything."

Curiosity got the better of me, and, over the next few days, I read a few articles on these so called "Mom Wars." It seemed a little like Waterloo. From what I could tell, no one was really winning, but if a clear loser were to emerge, civility would look a lot like Napoleon. The casualties were heavy on both sides. Moms who worked neglected their kids. Moms who stayed home ate bon bons and had attachment issues. Both armies were quick to load the cannons with shrapnel in the form of words like, "lazy," "career driven," and "nut." One set of women laid into each other so violently over bento boxes that I hit the deck before I could be decapitated by harpoons made of quinoa and indignation. But, just as things seemed darkest, all was not lost. In the melee, I was able to pick out a common thread winding its way through the smoke and dust. And it looked like a large group of people trying to prove two things, dedication and productivity.

At that moment, everything became clearer to me:

Moms who worked didn't have anyone standing over them, measuring how much they loved their kids during the day.

Moms who stayed home didn't have a designated person who gauged their productivity from eight to five.

Quickly, I called the local news station and asked for the producer.

"Yes, if you could just patch me through."

"But it's important."

"No, I don't have a publicist."

"I've figured it out! Don't you see? We're all doing the best we can. The only working mom who should be ridiculed is the one who picks her kids up and then makes them go rob a bank, while she waits in the getaway van. Stay-at-home moms need to be left alone, unless they're found wandering around on the lawn, mumbling about quarterly reports while the house burns down behind them. The greater metro area needs to know, if we're contributing to the health and well-being of our families, what we do has value."

"Oh."

"You're in craft services?"

"I see."

"And you don't have kids?"

"Uh huh."

"But could you make me a sandwich?"

"Hello?"

I never got my sandwich, but I did gain perspective. What I do may not be a "job," but it is *work*. In the past five years, I've wizened up and dropped my pursuit of having to feel productive in order to feel value. In twenty years, my success won't be measured in dishes done or floors scrubbed. On the other side of the coin, I listen to how hard my mom friends grind through the hours of the week at their various places of employment, and have nothing but respect for how they work tirelessly to keep finances flowing, kids bathed, and relish the time spent with their babies.

To devalue the two walks of life is silly. We're all working toward a common goal from different, and, most of the time, necessary angles. After all, life is unpredictable. I was never going to get married. I was never going to stay home. To say that I'll never be a working mom again is far from accurate because I simply don't know what's in the cards. But I do know one thing…

I'll do my best keeping the beer folded and the laundry cold, for as long as I'm here.

To Follow the Weekly Adventures
of Paige Kellerman, Please Visit:
www.paigekellerman.com

Other Books by Paige Kellerman:

At Least My Belly Hides My Cankles:
Mostly True Tales of An Impending Miracle

***

Acknowledgments

When I wrote the introduction to this book, I had a toddler sitting on top of me. For consistency's sake, a toddler is now standing on my lap and force feeding me fruit snacks, while I write a few notes of gratitude. Books don't pop into existence by themselves, and this one is no different. A beautiful team of people helped me put this labor of love together. A giant thanks to Scott Brooks, the mega-talented artist who took time out of doing much bigger projects to design the gorgeous cover of this book. More of Scott's stunning work can be found at www.drawbrooks.com. Another big thank you to my editor, Brenda Errichiello. You had the unenviable task of cleaning up my writing, and I'm truly grateful for your skill, humor, and attention to detail. Now, go hide before I ask you more questions.

To my beta readers, Christina, Heather, and Jolie, you guys are like sweet angels sent from heaven. Thank you for being faithful friends and sticking with me from the very beginning. Your support and hilarious messages helped me see another book through to the end, and your encouragement was invaluable on the days I wanted to be lazy, not write, and have a staring contest with the cat, instead. The same goes for my good friend, Abby Heugel. Thank you for writing the fabulous back copy of this book and being a true friend through the thick and thin of this writing journey. Abby is one of the funniest people I know. You can find her at www.abbyhasissues.com. To HBU and my countless other friends who have supported me over the years, thank you.

Last, but certainly not least, thank you to the wonderful man I call Husband and all my beautiful kids. Without you, there wouldn't be any books to speak of. I'd still be in insurance, wondering whether mold was covered and how many squirrels it takes to damage a wood roof. Thank you for putting up with me and all the frozen pizza. I love you more than anything.